THINK LIFE

HOLISTIC & HONORABLE

MUKESH DAILY

To the heartbeat of my existence,
My Parents

Smt. Patasi Devi & Late Shri Sanwar Mal

Contents

Contents

Think Life

Holistic & Honorable

Why

Nations will control you for Power.

Markets will exploit you for Wealth.

Religions will fool you for Influence.

Societies will trap you for Status.

What

Body of a Warrior, Mind of a Sage,

Heart of an Artist, Soul of a Monk.

How

Train like a Warrior, Think like a Sage,

Create like an Artist, Be like a Monk.

Think Life is like a roadmap for a meaningful journey through life in a holistic & honorable way. It's divided into four sections: Self, Family, World and God.

I. Self : Holistic & Honorable.

Let's start with the Self, where you're encouraged to be a superhero in your own story. It's not about doing a million things; it's about leading your life with the strength of character and being awesome in your physical, intellectual, creative and spiritual dimensions.

II. Family : Provide & Protect.

Now shift the focus to Family. It's like a warm hug from the universe emphasizing the importance of providing and protecting. Brotherhood, here, is like a cozy blanket on a chilly day, reminding you that you're not alone in this grand adventure.

III. World : Power & Control.

As we zoom out to the World, it's a bit like looking at a giant puzzle. Power and control play their roles in societies, religions, markets and nations. But guess what? You're not just a piece; you're a key player in the puzzle. Your choices matter in this vast interconnected game.

IV. God : Pray & Meditation.

Lastly, the God section is like a gentle breeze of hope and belief. The universe stretches before us an unexplored canvas full of mysteries. Prayer and meditation are like a soulful playlist that helps you tune into the rhythm of the divine.

Imagine it as your favorite song, each part adding its unique melody to the symphony of your existence.

A Note on How to Read

When you dive into this book, you've got to get the context, you know?
Otherwise, we're gonna find ourselves way out there at the two opposite
ends of the paradox spectrum.

Life is life, nature is nature and the world is just, well, the world. By the
textbook definitions, they're straightforward concepts.

But we live in a paradoxical world, my friend. Yep, these things, life,
nature and the world, they're all chock-full of paradoxical elements. On
the surface, they seem clear-cut but the deeper you go, the more you
realize there's a whole lot more to it. It's a wild ride, this thing called life.
So, when you look at life, it's important to see both sides of the coin.

CHAPTER ONE

LIFE IS A PARADOX

A Note on Civilized & Ruthless People.

Life is a paradox, My friend. You must be a good person and a dangerous person.

It's a hard truth of our world that the powerful prey upon the weak. Justice, unfortunately, comes after someone has already suffered as a victim. It's a grim reality that those seeking justice must take up the fight themselves. But why wait for injustice to befall you? It's far wiser to take proactive steps to minimize the chances of becoming a victim. The responsibility to ensure your safety and security ultimately falls on your shoulders. True justice, as we envision it, can sometimes be an elusive concept. True justice will never be served. That's a tragic concept.

Let's be clear about one thing: the government isn't responsible for the safety of individuals. Yes, it can create a safe environment, deliver justice and even take revenge in certain situations, especially in cases involving enemy countries. However, when it comes to the safety of yourself and your family, you must be the first line of defense. There's no knight in shining armor coming to your rescue. Only you have the power to protect yourself and those you care about. It's important to face this reality head on. So, wake up to the responsibility that rests on your shoulders. Nobody will save you. Only you can.

I've got a question for you and it's an important one. Can you honestly say that you're prepared to protect yourself and your family from all kinds of potential attacks? Chances are, for most of us, the answer is a resounding "no". But why is that? The simple truth is, we just haven't given it much thought.

We've spent so much time thinking about a myriad of other things in our lives but we've somehow managed to overlook the very real threats to our existence. It's a bit mind boggling when you stop and think about it. Most of us are likely to live anywhere from 60 to 100 years and in that time we're bound to come face to face with some pretty daunting, life threatening situations. And here's the kicker: our children and their children are likely to face these challenges too.

Take a look around you. Millions of people are already dealing with these threats every day and that should serve as a stark reminder that none of us are invincible. So let's start thinking about our safety and the well being of our loved ones. It's time to get prepared because, in the complex world, we're all just a bit more vulnerable than we might like to admit.

Study history extensively. Analyze who emerged victorious and who suffered defeat. Even if the victim eventually triumphed, they often suffered immense losses. Throughout history, good people have endured tremendous suffering. Most of our great leaders and ideals were initially victims and they persevered through prolonged struggles for justice. It's essential to fight for justice but it's equally important to be resilient and proactive to avoid becoming victims.

I want to talk to you about a tragic chapter in the history of India, the Exodus of Kashmiri Pandits. This is a story of a community forced to leave their homeland due to an extreme climate of fear, violence and ruthless persecution.

The Kashmiri Pandits, a Hindu minority group in the Kashmir Valley, have a rich and ancient history in the region, tracing their roots back thousands of years. For centuries, they lived in the beauty and tranquility of the Vale of Kashmir with relative peace and harmony. The Kashmiri Pandits community was known for their knowledge, wisdom, compassion, love and worship of god.

However, in the late 1980s and early 1990s, this peace was shattered by a surge of insurgency and terrorism in the region. Militant groups with alleged support from across the border launched a campaign of violence and intimidation that targeted the Kashmiri Pandit community.

The situation deteriorated rapidly and they were subjected to threats, violence and coercion. Kashmiri Pandits never believed in violence. They never picked the guns. They thought the government would save them. It lead to the Kashmiri Pandit Genocide. As a result over a short period 100,000+ of the Kashmiri Pandits were forced to flee their homes, leaving behind their ancestral land, culture and way of life.

The exodus of Kashmiri Pandits was a human tragedy of immense proportions. Families were torn apart, livelihoods were lost and a rich cultural heritage was left in jeopardy. The pain and trauma of that period continue to haunt the displaced community to this day.

Justice was never served. They never returned to their homes in the Kashmir Valley. Truly there is no equivalent justice for genocides.

History is filled with great tragedies, present is being filled with great tragedies. It's not just about one story, there are millions of other tragic stories of good people. It's our responsibility to shape a better future, one where we are not victims but architects of our destiny.

If one holds a book in one hand, one must also hold a gun in the other. Anything of value must be protected. We take extreme precaution of our wealth, locked and well protected. What about the most precious of all - Human Lives? It is unfortunate that people neither have the right to have guns to protect themselves, nor the government will protect them. Justice requires you to become a victim first. And Justice is not guaranteed.

On one hand, life can be so incredibly fragile. I mean, think about it. Our time on this planet is limited and we're not here forever. But on the other hand, life is resilient. It's this force of nature that keeps pushing forward, adapting to challenges and finding a way to survive and thrive. It's this relentless spirit that never gives up.

And then there's the fact that life is both predictable and unpredictable. We make plans, set goals and try to control our destiny but sometimes life throws us these curveballs, surprises us in the most unexpected ways.

Life is also a mix of joy and sorrow. We experience moments of pure happiness but we also face pain and heartache. It's this rollercoaster of emotions that takes us from the highest highs to the lowest lows. Life is a complex and contradictory journey that we're all on and that's what makes it so incredibly fascinating and worth living to the fullest. Embrace the paradox and you'll find the true magic of life.

Life is a paradox, My friend. You must be a good person and a dangerous person.

CHAPTER TWO

WORLD IS A PARADOX

A Note on Societies, Religions, Markets & Nations.

World is a paradox, my friend. It's this vast, complex place where you've got society, religion, the market and nations - they're all part of this puzzle that doesn't quite fit together smoothly. It's a complex web of contradictions, where you've got to navigate your way through the beauty and the chaos, the unity and the division and try to make sense of it all.

Society is a paradox of cooperation and conflict. Society is a place where diverse cultures, ideas and people come together to create something amazing. But at the same time it is also a source of division and conflict.

On one hand, it was formed for our survival, to promote cooperation, to watch each other's backs. It was an idea where we all come together, cooperate and thrive. Flip that coin and you'll see the conflicts. Extreme selfishness is on the rise and that sense of community has become a thing of the past. Greed has taken the center stage at the cost of others. Everyone is always focused on getting ahead rather than on helping out. It has become a competition till death.

It has become a game of status and show off. People are out there, flaunting their success, their possessions which have nothing to do with what truly matters in life. And then there's the whole individuality thing. Instead of celebrating our uniqueness, sometimes society pushes us to conform, to suppress our individuality. Diversity? Well, it should be a strength but where is the acceptance!

Religion is a paradox of enlightenment and ignorance. It's this deeply personal, spiritual journey for many, filled with faith, values and a sense of purpose. But it's also been a source of strife and division throughout history.

Religion can be a force for social good. Many use it as a driving force to help those in need, to make the world a better place. But and this is a big "but", it can also get twisted for extremism and violence.

On one hand, it's this beautiful force that brings people together, forging connections. But on the other hand, it can be manipulated for all sorts of things. Some people use it to fool others and it's like this dark side of faith that leads people astray.

Market is a paradox of wealth and poverty. It's a dynamic force of supply and demand where you've got commerce and trade driving innovation and prosperity. But it's also a place where inequality and greed runs rampant.

On one hand, they're a hub of creativity and opportunity.. They drive progress, create jobs and fuel economic growth. But then, there's that flip side. Businesses are getting pretty ruthless, where profit is the one and only goal at the expense of the well-being of the public. This drive for financial gain leads to exploitation, promoting consumerism and prioritizing the bottom line over everything else.

Public well being has taken a backseat in the pursuit of profit. It's a paradox, really, where on one hand, you've got the potential for amazing progress and on the other a potential for exploitation and the loss of what's truly valuable.

Nation is a paradox of sovereignty and slavery. These political entities that define our borders and identities bring unity, pride and sovereignty but nations are also at the center of conflicts and power struggles in a race to control the lives of individuals.

Nations, on one hand, are there to protect their people, ensuring our survival through cooperation. It's about coming together as a society to keep us safe and thriving. But then, there's the darker side. governments exploit their own people and that's a harsh truth. They wield power and control in the name of serving us, sometimes they go to great lengths to keep a grip on the population. Corruption runs rampant in some places and the common good isn't always at the top of the agenda - it's power and control that take the front seat.

And, let's talk about freedom – it feels like this distant concept in some corners of the world. You've got governments that should be serving the people but instead they tighten the reins, limit our freedoms and it's a constant tug-of-war between the rulers and the ruled. It's a real paradox, this whole thing. On one side it's about protection and cooperation but on the other it's a power struggle, a messy mix of service and control, where the line between the two can get all blurry.

CHAPTER THREE

NATURE IS A PARADOX

A Note on Creation & Destruction, Beauty & Brutality.

Nature is a paradox, my friend. It's this constant tug-of-war between creation and destruction and it's happening all around us, all the time. It's an ongoing epic battle between the forces of life and death.

It's got its wild side and it's not always gentle. You've got these beautiful, gentle rain showers that can make you feel so at peace with the world. The way those droplets fall, the soothing sound it makes and how it nourishes the earth, it's a sight to behold. But then nature's like, "Hold on a sec" and sends a storm our way. Lightning, thunder and torrents of rain.

Now, take the jungle. You wander into it and you're surrounded by this lush, vibrant beauty. The trees, the animals, the whole ecosystem, it's a beautiful masterpiece itself. It's all serene and picturesque, right? But in that very same jungle, there's a brutality that's just as real. It's a battleground where survival is a fierce game and every creature is in it to win it. It's a ruthless, survival-of-the-fittest kinda deal, where creatures have to fight tooth and nail just to make it. So, on one hand, you've got this serene, picturesque scene and on the other, it's a cutthroat competition. It's both peaceful and fierce at the same time.

When it comes to natural disasters, nature pulls no punches. Earthquakes are like the planet's way of saying "I've got some power to unleash". The ground shakes, buildings crumble and it's pure destruction. And then there are tsunamis, those monstrous waves that can sweep entire coastlines away. It's a brutal, heart-wrenching force, a show of nature's relentless power. They can strike at any moment, often without warning and they have the ability to cause widespread devastation and loss of life. These are forces of nature that are beyond human control and can unleash unimaginable power.

We live in a positive thinking world where we only like to see the one side of a coin, history is filled with natural disasters where millions of people lost their lives together.

The 1931 China Floods took millions of lives, making it one of the deadliest natural disasters in history.

The 2004 Indian Ocean Tsunami triggered by an undersea earthquake off the coast of Sumatra, Indonesia, impacted many countries and resulted in over 230,000 casualties, making it one of the deadliest tsunamis in recorded history.

The 1815 Mount Tambora Eruption in Indonesia is the most powerful volcanic eruption in recorded history. This explosion sent so much volcanic ash into the atmosphere that it caused a "Year Without a Summer" in 1816.

The 2010 Haiti earthquake was a catastrophic magnitude 7.0 Mw earthquake that devastated the capital claiming approximately 300,000 lives.

The 1755 Lisbon Earthquake struck the city of Lisbon, Portugal, in the 18th century. It was one of the most powerful quakes ever recorded in Europe, estimated to be around magnitude 9.0. The tremors followed by a massive tsunami and fires almost completely destroyed Lisbon.

The 1900 Galveston Hurricane was the deadliest hurricane in U.S. history that struck the city of Galveston, Texas. It resulted in the loss of an estimated 8,000 lives and nearly wiped out the city.

It's this never-ending cycle of creation and destruction, beauty and brutality, life and death and it keeps us on our toes.

I. Self: Holistic & Honorable

Self is limitless, Identity is limiting.

Let's start with the Self, where you're a superhero in your own story. It's not about doing a million things; it's about leading your life with the strength of character and being awesome in your physical, intellectual, creative and spiritual dimensions.

CHAPTER FOUR

Character

Authenticity defines character, Integrity shapes character, Character defines you.

There are billions of people in the world but there is only one you and that's pretty amazing if you ask me. The idea that you're unlike anyone else out there, that your experiences, your thoughts, your body - they're all uniquely yours. And that's something to be celebrated! Don't be afraid to let your unique self shine, let your authentic self be the best version of you. It's the things that make you different that can make you truly remarkable. That's not something to be suppressed.

Our individuality is what gives us our own flavor, our own style, our own perspective on the world. It's what makes us stand out in a crowd and it's what makes life interesting and diverse. Embrace your individuality, My Friend. Don't be afraid to be yourself, to express your thoughts, your feelings, your quirks. It's what sets you apart, what makes you, well, you. And that's a wonderful thing.

So, don't try to conform to some preconceived notion of what you should be. Be proud of who you are and let your individuality shine. It's what makes the world a more colorful and exciting place. Society benefits from this diversity. Our individuality allows us to excel in various fields and to come up with innovative ideas. Every single one of us brings something unique to the table. Our individuality, our distinct personalities, our talents and our perspectives, they all contribute to the society at large. It's like a puzzle where every piece, no matter how different, has a role to play in creating the big picture.

Unfortunately society is moving towards suppressing individuality. They need conformists, which are no more than sheep. It's your duty to create a society that values individual opinions and allows people to express their unique views. Not everything is served to you. Not everything will be served to your future generations.

You are different, Your values are different, Your mindset is different, Your character is different. Things can be copied and created but you, yourself, is unique. So keep it that way. You are unique.

I'll share a lot of things for reference, it will teach you nothing but if you can relate, it will reveal you. Ultimately you will design your own life.

You might ask why character is important or does it even matter? To answer that you should look at character in a holistic way, you should also consider what is a weak character and a strong character. Why holistic, because if you don't look at it in a holistic way then someone will measure your character with their scale. Markets will measure you with how much you help them make money. Religion will measure you with how religious you are. Nation will measure you with how obedient a citizen you are. And obviously Society will measure you with status. What I am asking is that you must measure your character in your scale, your values, your authenticity and your integrity - who you are. Everyone else will have their definition of you. Let's begin with the character that defines us.

Have you ever stopped to admire the majestic character of the eagle?

Eagles are such remarkable creatures, they love storms. The way they brace the harshest weather conditions and emerge unscathed, that's a testament to their inner fortitude, no storm in life is too fierce for them.

Their fearlessness is awe-inspiring! Eagles fear nothing when they hunt or protect their territory. Eagles fiercely protect their nests and young ones from predators.

Eagles have remarkable vision. With their keen eyesight, they spot prey from incredible distances. which serves as a metaphor for having a clear and focused vision in life.

Eagles are solitary birds, capable of self-reliance. Eagles are known for their loyalty to their mate, often forming lifelong bonds.

The story of the eagle is a living masterpiece, reminding us of the strength of character that lies within us.

Our character acts like a lighthouse, casting a steady beam upon the sea of moral choices. It's the compass that directs us toward the shores of our values, unwavering in the midst of the most seductive storms. When challenges arise, it is the strength of our character that fortifies us, enabling us to navigate life's twists and turns with resilience and courage. It ensures that we remain true to our values even when faced with difficult choices.

Character is like a beautifully crafted sculpture that's both one-of-a-kind and strong in its values.

Authenticity takes the lead, defining the character with a touch of uniqueness and genuineness. It's about being true to oneself, about letting your true colors shine through your actions and interactions. Authenticity creates the distinct identity that makes your character stand out.

Integrity comes next, shaping the character's core. It emphasizes ethics and unwavering moral principles. Like a strong and reliable framework, integrity lays the groundwork for the character's strength and resilience.

When integrity and authenticity come together, they form a powerful partnership. They cultivate a character that is both strong, genuine and one-of-a-kind. They're the dynamic duo that molds and sculpts, ensuring that your character is not only authentic but also shaped with a solid and ethical foundation.

Remember character is not static. It is a lifelong work in progress. It has the capacity to grow and transform as we journey through life.

A Politician, An Intellectual, A Businessman, A Common Citizen will have values that are often in conflict with each other. Behold these fundamental and holistic values, a compass to guide yourself and your interactions with others, for honor's timeless embrace.

Values

Love

Love is Eternal, Passion is Fleeting.

Honor & Respect

Honorable Life, Respectful Bonds.

Courage & Wisdom

Wisdom Guides, Courage Achieves.

Perseverance & Resilience

Perseverance strengthens, Resilience endures.

Freedom & Liberty

Freedom of Mind & Liberty of Soul.

Truth & Justice

Truth Triumphs, Justice Prevails.

Strength & Power

Strength yields Power, Power molds Destinies.

Empathy & Compassion

Empathy Unites, Compassion Heals.

Humility & Gratitude

If you don't value what you have, you'll never value what you'll get.

～

Love

Love is Eternal, Passion is Fleeting.

पोथी पढ़ि पढ़ि जग मुआ, पंडित भया न कोय ।

ढाई आख़र प्रेम का, पढ़े सो पंडित होय ।।

- कबीर दास

Translation:

Reading books everyone died, none became any wise
One who reads the word of Love, only becomes wise.

Wisdom does not blossom within the pages of books. The wise are those who understand the profound meaning of "Love". In the language of the

English, a term exists, "Passion". Yet, passion pales before the boundless expanse of Love. Love is Eternal. Love, the eternal essence, is the radiant seed of existence.

Love precedes all; Knowledge follows in its wake. Love is first, Knowledge is secondary. Knowledge without love won't produce magnificent art.

Let me lay it out for you plain and simple: when it comes to creating great art, love is the secret sauce. No amount of technical know-how can make up for the absence of genuine love for the craft. I mean, think about it. You might be a walking encyclopedia of art knowledge but if your heart isn't in it, how can you possibly expect to produce something truly exceptional?

Love, my friend, that's what it's all about. If you're not head over heels in love with what you do, your creations will inevitably suffer. You can be the smartest cookie in the jar but if you're going through the motions without putting your heart into it, all that intelligence doesn't count for much.

And here's the thing about love: it's not something you can learn or acquire. You can study and gain knowledge, sure, but you can't teach yourself to love. Love is that elusive, magical ingredient that breathes life into your work. So, if you want to create something truly remarkable, let that love guide your hand and watch your art come alive in ways you never thought possible.

Love precedes all; Courage comes as an accompaniment. Love is first, Courage is secondary. For a mother's valor in protecting her offspring is not borne of courage but Love. The biggest, boldest and most unwavering courage comes from love. When you love something or someone with all your heart, it's like a fire burning inside you and you'd do whatever it takes to protect it, no matter the cost.

You see, love has this incredible power to push us to the limits, to take us to places we never thought possible. It's a force that makes us willing to go to any length and travel any distance to safeguard what we hold dear. Love is the driving force behind some of the most remarkable acts of bravery and sacrifice in the world. Love is the ultimate source of unwavering bravery.

Love is the Seed, Love is Eternal. Without Love, life unfolds as a relentless toil. But with Love, each endeavor transforms into a joyous play.

"All, everything that I understand, I understand only because I love." - Leo Tolstoy

~

Honor & Respect

Honorable Life, Respectful Bonds.

Honor is a sacred promise we make to ourselves, a bond with our own character that we must never break. When we choose honor, we choose to live with principle, knowing that our word is our bond and our actions a testament to our convictions.

Respect is the bridge that connects hearts and minds, forging connections that endure the test of time. When we offer respect, we create a world where differences are celebrated and people are treated with grace and dignity.

Your life is better for being a certain kind of person than it is for having certain kinds of things. Honorable is the way, not an achievement. Your behavior reflects your upbringing.

True power is not in domination but in the strength of character. Honor the legacy of those who came before us and respect the companionship of those who walk beside us.

Honor is holistic. Let your words and deeds be trustworthy, avoiding the shadows of deceit and falsehood. Being a great achiever but deceiving the world, exploiting the weak and cheating on spouse is not Honorable.

Extend the hand of respect to all, regardless of their origins, beliefs or stature. In every interaction, let politeness, respect and consideration be your guiding principles.

The pages of life's story are turned with the wisdom of age. Showing reverence to those who have tread upon more chapters is not only a sign of respect but a tribute to the wisdom they bestow, It's honorable. Adorning oneself with attire that pays homage to the moment's significance is honorable.

Everyday acts of courtesy like holding the door open for someone, offering your seat to those in need and giving up your place in a line to someone with limited mobility is honorable.

It's not honorable to mock somebody, make jokes of somebody or speak bad about somebody. You may disagree but honor that person with your words. Avoiding unnecessary gossip and negative comments about others is honorable.

Courage & Wisdom

Wisdom Guides, Courage Achieves.

Blend the courage of a warrior with the wisdom of a sage and you can craft not only your own destinies but the fate of humanity itself.

Courage empowers us to face the unknown, while wisdom acts as our trusted guide, whispering the lessons of experience and knowledge. In the face of adversity, courage is the roaring thunder that drowns out the whispers of uncertainty, while wisdom serves as the compass of sound judgment.

Courage without wisdom may lead to reckless endeavors, while wisdom without courage can result in inaction and missed opportunities. Together, they form a harmonious partnership that enables us to traverse the unpredictable landscapes of life.

"Life shrinks or expands in proportion to one's courage." - Anais Nin

Perseverance & Resilience

Perseverance strengthens, Resilience endures.

Perseverance is the relentless force that whispers, "try again" when the world echoes "give up." Perseverance breathes life into our ambitions, molding them from mere desires into tangible realities. It is the heartbeat that propels us forward, unswayed by the storms that may rage. When we persist, we discover the heights to which we can soar, for perseverance strengthens the wings of our dreams, making them capable of flight.

Resilience endures and in that endurance, we thrive. It is the some form of hope that plays even in the darkest hours. When we cultivate resilience, we discover that there is no storm so fierce that it can extinguish the fire of our spirit. Like a phoenix rising, we are reborn from the embers of challenge and we emerge stronger, wiser and more powerful than before.

"Ever tried. Ever failed. No matter. Try again. Fail again. Fail better."- Samuel Beckett

History is filled with timeless examples of Perseverance and Resilience. Rana Sanga was a fierce Rajput king who was known for his courage and tenacity. He fought against the foreign invaders despite losing one arm, one eye and had close to 80 wounds on his body.

Maharana Pratap, Grandson of Rana Sanga, the 16th-century Rajput warrior king of Mewar, is a great example of unparalleled perseverance and resilience in the face of adversity. He was the eldest son of Maharana Udai Singh and was destined to be the ruler of Mewar. However, his reign was marked by challenges and external threats, primarily from the Mughal Empire under Emperor Akbar. The most critical turning point in Pratap's life was the Battle of Haldighati in 1576, where he faced Akbar's forces led by Man Singh. Despite being outnumbered and facing formidable opposition, Pratap and his loyal army fought valiantly. The battle ended inconclusively but it was a testament to Pratap's unyielding spirit and his refusal to submit to the Mughal Empire's authority.

After the Battle of Haldighati, Pratap and his loyal followers engaged in a protracted guerrilla warfare campaign in the rugged Aravalli hills. They relied on their knowledge of the terrain, hit-and-run tactics and their deep-seated commitment to Mewar's independence. Pratap faced numerous hardships, including scarcity of resources, harsh living conditions and the loss of territories but he never gave up. Maharana Pratap's steadfast resistance against the Mughals continued for decades. Despite the odds he remained true to his vow never to bow to Akbar. His resilience inspired his loyal subjects and earned him their unwavering support. Ultimately, Pratap's refusal to accept Mughal dominance laid the foundation for Mewar's continued independence and his legacy endures as a symbol of valor and resistance against foreign rule.

Freedom & Liberty

Freedom of Mind & Liberty of Soul.

Take a good, hard look at professional networking platforms and you'll see something quite interesting. On these platforms, employees often find themselves walking on eggshells, trying their best to align themselves with the expectations of potential employers. They're hesitant to express their minds freely and that's just a plain fact. And that right there is where we see the erosion of our freedom and liberty.

Now if you compare these professional platforms to other social ones, you'll spot a stark difference in how people interact. On those social platforms, people tend to open up and share their minds more freely.

It's a puzzling shift, isn't it? We should be able to express ourselves and have open discussions, especially when it comes to our professional lives. But when we start holding back, fearing the consequences of speaking our minds, we lose a piece of ourselves.

Every mind in the world is capable of boundless creativity and innovation.

The most beautiful melodies are composed by those who dare to be different, to think differently and to feel differently. Just as a soaring bird finds its truest liberty in the open sky, our souls find their most authentic expression when unburdened by societal norms and expectations.

Freedom of mind fuels our intellectual pursuits and liberty of soul sets the stage for our creative expressions. It is the key to unfettered expression of our individuality, celebration of the unique rhythm of each human being.

It allows our thoughts to traverse uncharted territories that lead to original thoughts, pushing the boundaries of knowledge and challenging the status quo.

To fight for these values is to champion the essence of our individuality, that enriches the world with the colors of uniqueness and originality.

"Liberty without thought is like a disturbed spirit." - Khalil Gibran

Truth & Justice

Truth Triumphs, Justice Prevails.

We've all encountered those folks who just can't seem to tell the truth, those we can't rely on. It's frustrating, isn't it? Once you've discerned that someone isn't truthful, it's hard to trust them. I've unfortunately come across many such individuals who repeatedly twist the facts.

Now, I get it, you can't simply sever ties with everyone who falls into this category but you sure can protect yourself by not taking their words at face value. We all have those people in our lives, the ones for whom deceit and betrayal is their nature.

You can't change their intrinsic nature but you can certainly make the choice to distance yourself. You can safeguard your own well-being or if necessary, respond decisively and in a way that's quantifiable. It's all about protecting yourself in a world where not everyone values truthfulness.

"Honesty is a very expensive gift, Don't expect it from cheap people." - Warren Buffett

Now don't discard the concept of truthfulness by applying it in a different context. In a normal day to day setting you deal with common people in your life and not the enemies.

The history is filled with countless examples, where deceit and falsehood often attempted to obscure the clarity of Truth. Yet there's a fire within the human spirit that refuses to yield.

Truth is the unwavering beacon of our moral compass. Truth transcends the borders of deceit and falsehood. It is the bedrock upon which trust is built. It's a bridge connecting hearts and minds.

The pursuit of truth calls upon us to seek knowledge to discern fact from fiction and to stand firm in the face of dishonesty. Truth illuminates the darkest corners, dispels ignorance and upholds the values of integrity and enlightenment.

Justice is the faithful companion of truth, it's the guardian of fairness and equality. It is the timeless value that ensures that wrongs are righted and that every individual is treated with equality and respect.

This anthem "Truth Triumphs, Justice Prevails" reminds us that, no matter what, the power of truth and justice will endure. It stands as a symbol of hope for humanity, a promise for a better world where transgressions will not go unchecked and that righteousness shall prevail.

Of course we have to fight. In the relentless struggle for Truth and Justice, we rise above the shadows, undaunted by adversity, resolute in the face of deception. We become the architects of a world where lies are defeated and fairness reigns. It is a value worth upholding and fighting for.

In all your dealings, aspire to be just and impartial, banishing discrimination, prejudice and unfairness from your life.

"Injustice anywhere is a threat to justice everywhere." - Martin Luther King Jr.

Strength & Power

Strength yields Power, Power molds Destinies.

क्षमा शोभती उस भुजंग को जिसके पास गरल हो
उसको क्या जो दंतहीन विषरहित, विनीत, सरल हो।
- Ramdhari Singh Dinkar

Translation:

Forgiveness adorns that serpent who possesses venom. None cares for the toothless, poisonless, kind, gentle one.

Use your strength and power for good, be kind to helpless but let not our enemies perceive our kindness as a vulnerability to exploit. Instead, they should remember us for our unwavering commitment to what we hold dear. When faced with an adversary, stand firm and resolute in your convictions.

Strength is not merely the capacity to lift heavy weights or overcome physical challenges. It is the courage to face the unknown, to stand tall in the face of adversity and to conquer the battles. It is the unyielding determination that refuses to bow to the weight of life's burdens. It is the unbreakable resolve that says, "I will not be defeated".

Power is the ability to channel that strength to harness and direct it towards a purpose. It is the force that moves mountains, that changes the course of history, that shapes destinies. Power is the realization that one's actions have the potential to make a profound impact on the world and the responsibility that comes with it.

Find balance where the open heart and the unwavering spirit coexist harmoniously, forging a path towards a world where healing is abundant and resilience is impenetrable.

Strength and power are not reserved for the select few or the born leaders. We are all born with the potential for greatness and it is up to us to unlock it.

Strength and power are not the end goals in themselves. They are the means to achieve something greater and it is in the wise and compassionate use of these gifts that true greatness is achieved. They are the tools that allow us to protect and to effect positive change in the world.

Akbar, the third Mughal emperor of India, is a great example of remarkable strength and power that reshaped the course of Indian history during the 16th century.

Akbar was a formidable strategist and commander. He expanded his empire through a series of successful military campaigns, including the conquest of northern and central India. Akbar's army was known for its strength and discipline and he skillfully incorporated artillery into his campaigns, giving him a technological advantage. Akbar's reign demonstrated not just physical power but also the power of diplomacy and statecraft. He forged strategic alliances and established a far-reaching empire.

"I'm a kind person, I'm kind to everyone, but if you are unkind to me, then kindness is not what you'll remember me for." - Al Capone

Good people don't want power but when bad actors misuse power, they become victims. Power isn't good or bad in itself. Power in the good hands can shape a better world.

Empathy & Compassion

Empathy Unites, Compassion Heals.

Empathy is listening to understand others emotions and perspectives. Compassion is the desire to take action to help the helpless.

People often misunderstand compassion, misapplying it in inappropriate contexts and using it to address their personal issues that may require a different approach. In doing so, they mistakenly attribute all their problems to compassion. Compassion is not the cure for everything.

World is full of psychopaths who are interested only in ruthlessly self serving. If you want a more humane and harmonious society for yourself and your future generations, then that world can only be built on empathy, understanding and love.

In a world often marked by division and discord, empathy serves as a powerful antidote. It bridges the gaps between us, transcending boundaries of race, religion and nationality. It unites us all in our common humanity.

It takes courage to open our hearts and extend a helping hand. It's the driving force behind countless acts of kindness and selflessness that make the world a better place.

Our words can be incredibly powerful and we should handle them with care. They might just be the last words someone ever hears. We all are mortal and the truth is we could leave this world at any moment. In the hustle and bustle of life, when people are still with us, we tend to do all sorts of silly things. We say things we don't mean, we quarrel, we fight and we sometimes let the trivialities of life take over.

You'll never regret the kind words you said to someone. But you'll surely regret it if you said something hurtful and that person is no longer here the next day. It's possible that we may not have the opportunity to see them tomorrow. Life is fragile. Life is not forever. Don't let harsh words or thoughtless actions define your interactions with others. Let me share with you a remarkable story of compassion that goes in the history as one of the greatest.

In the bustling streets of Calcutta, there lived a remarkable woman, Mother Teresa. In her presence, the forsaken found a refuge, the broken discovered healing and the disheartened glimpsed hope. Mother Teresa dedicated her entire life to serving the poorest of the poor, the sick and the suffering in the streets of Calcutta and beyond. Her actions were a living embodiment of compassion, a force that transcended words and touched the very core of human existence.

She once said, ***"It's not how much we give but how much love we put into giving."*** This encapsulates her philosophy of compassion. It wasn't just about providing material aid; it was about offering love, dignity and respect to those who had been marginalized and forgotten.

Mother Teresa's compassion was not limited by religious or cultural boundaries. She believed in the universality of compassion, that it's a language understood by all. Regardless of our faith or background, we can all appreciate the simple yet profound act of extending a hand to someone in need. She showed us that compassion isn't always about grand gestures or monumental acts. It can be found in the smallest of deeds and the gentlest of words. It's in the kindness we show to a stranger, the patience we offer to someone in pain and the love we share with those who have none.

Mother Teresa's life is a beautiful example of how love and compassion can make a big difference in the world. It's a great example that compassion is not just an abstract concept; it's a living, breathing force that can transform the world. It's a force that can heal, unite and uplift humanity.

Humility & Gratitude

If you don't value what you have, you'll never value what you'll get.

We've all had the experience of lending a helping hand to someone time and time again, only to find that gratitude is a foreign concept to them. We've all had the experience of meeting people whose ego is bigger than the cosmos. How do you feel about those people? Most likely you don't want to be like any of them and you don't want any of them in your life.

Humility is a quality that speaks volumes. It's all about staying down to earth, showing respect and recognizing that no matter how far you've come, you care about others. It's the kind of trait that resonates with people and makes you stand out in the best way possible.

If your only goal is personal success, then that's a whole different story. But if you want to connect with people and make a difference, humility is your key to unlock that door. You can't be a social leader without humility.

Gratitude, My Friend, is a powerful notion that we often forget in the hustle and bustle of our lives. Think about it for a moment.

No matter who you are, in the grand cosmos you are just a tiny speck, a minuscule dot on a dot in the vast universe. You don't have any control over nature and you can't even comprehend or control the internal workings of your own body. In the grand scheme of things we are nobody. We are nothing.

Think about the countless forces at play to keep you firmly in your place and to sustain your existence. The Earth itself provides you with a habitat and abundant resources. Trees generously give you life sustaining oxygen, the air you breathe. Who are you, really?

Now, consider the people who brought you into this world your father and your mother. Have you ever stopped to think about the sacrifices they made for you? Their love, care and guidance? It's a privilege that not everyone enjoys. There are individuals out there who don't have the opportunity to express their gratitude to their parents. I hope you have.

If you take a moment to look at the world around you, you'll see the interconnectedness of life. Have some gratitude for the world we live in and the people who make our lives better.

People who have no gratitude for anything in life are mean people, They aren't worth spending time with as they will take away everything you have to offer without even expressing the gratitude.

A simple act of saying **thank you** can shape your relationship with the world, yourself and god. It's a reflection of your character.

Mindset

Your mindset is a direct result of your established beliefs, attitudes and thought patterns that shape your perception of yourself, others and the world around you. It plays a significant role in influencing your behavior, your decisions and your responses to various situations.

Mindset is not something that is fixed forever; it must evolve and change over time based on your experiences, learning and intentional efforts. Some mindset will hold you back, while some will move you forward. So it's a good idea to at least have an idea of what mindset is. It will help you understand why your choices are the way they are.

Here I am sharing a list of different types of mindset as a quick reminder. Just ask yourself, in different situations, which mindset you are in.

According to a situation it's wise to be in the best suited mindset. Remember life is a paradox. You don't want to be open minded when someone is fooling you. Use your critical thinking and only you can decide what is best for you in the given situation.

Fixed vs Growth

One of the most well known distinctions in mindset is the fixed mindset vs growth mindset. A fixed mindset believes that abilities and intelligence are inherent and unchangeable while a growth mindset sees them as malleable and capable of improvement through effort and learning.

Positive vs Negative

A positive mindset tends to focus on opportunities, solutions and optimism, whereas a negative mindset tends to emphasize problems, obstacles and pessimism.

Open vs Closed

An open mindset is receptive to new ideas, experiences and perspectives, while a closed mindset tends to be resistant to change and new information.

Proactive vs Reactive

A proactive mindset takes initiatives and responsibility for one's life and actions while a reactive mindset tends to respond to external events and circumstances.

Abundance vs Scarcity

An abundance mindset sees the world as full of opportunities and resources while a scarcity mindset focuses on limitations and a lack of resources.

Self limiting vs Empowering

A self-limiting mindset can hold an individual back through self-doubt, fear and a sense of inadequacy while an empowering mindset promotes self-confidence, resilience and a belief in one's own abilities.

Fixed Beliefs vs Open Beliefs

A mindset can be defined by the rigidity or flexibility of an individual's beliefs and opinions. Some people have fixed, unchanging beliefs while others are open to revising their beliefs based on new information and experiences.

Risk Averse vs Risk Tolerant

A risk-averse mindset avoids uncertainty and potential failure while a risk-tolerant mindset embraces challenges and sees failures as opportunities for growth.

Problem Oriented vs Solution Oriented

Some mindsets focus primarily on problems while others seek out solutions and possibilities.

How To Develop A Strong Mindset

Self Awareness

You know, you and I, we're far from perfect. But there are many people out there who seem to be in a perpetual state of confusion. They're constantly baffled by their own selves, not having a clue about what they truly desire, what they hold dear and what they stand for. One moment, they're on this side of the fence and the next they've jumped over to the other side. These individuals end up being taken for a ride by just about anyone in the world and they're left scratching their heads, wondering what went wrong. The root of their problem? It's a glaring lack of self awareness. It takes experience, it takes time.

Self awareness is the journey within ourselves where we seek to understand who we truly are, what motivates us and how we fit into the world around us. It involves taking a long and hard look at ourselves, our strengths, our weaknesses, our values and our beliefs. But why is self awareness so important, you might ask?

To grow, we must know where we stand. Self awareness is the mirror that reflects our current state. With this knowledge, we can set realistic goals, work on our weaknesses and build on our strengths. When we know our values and what truly matters to us, we can make choices that align with our authentic selves. This leads to a sense of purpose and fulfillment in our lives.

Self awareness helps us recognize our emotions and how they impact our decisions and interactions with others. When we understand why we feel the way we do, we can better manage our emotional responses. It's not just about understanding ourselves; it's also about understanding how we affect those around us. Self-awareness enhances our empathy and communication skills leading to healthier, more fulfilling relationships.

The beauty of self-awareness lies in its transformative power. It's the key to unlocking your true potential and living a life that's more meaningful and authentic. It's through self awareness you will design your own life.

Understanding your own beliefs, attitudes and thought patterns is important for developing a growth mindset. Self-awareness allows you to identify areas where your mindset may be limiting you and take steps to change it. Core beliefs and values play a significant role in shaping your mindset. These are deeply ingrained and can influence how you perceive the world and yourself.

Life Experiences

There's this memorable line from the movie Magnificent Seven that really hits home. It goes something like:

"Well, the graveyards are full of boys who were very young and very proud".

In today's world, we see so many young folks out there, especially on social media, proudly touting their success and knowledge. But the thing about this kind of knowledge is that it's often as fleeting as their success. It's like a shooting star, bright for a moment but then gone in an instant.

Real wisdom, the kind that's all encompassing and enduring, well, that comes with age and experience. It's not something you can brag about on a social media post; it's the kind of wisdom that's quietly accumulated over time.

Life is about experiencing. Experiences give life its depth and meaning. They are the source of our most profound moments of fulfillment and happiness. Experiences are what shapes our lives, change us and leave an indelible mark on our souls. Our lives are a collection of experiences, each one unique, irreplaceable and invaluable.

Experiences are our greatest teachers. They impart wisdom, knowledge and life lessons that no classroom or textbook can ever provide. It's through experiences that we truly grow and evolve. Every new experience broadens our perspective. It enables us to see the world through different lenses and better our understanding of others.

Each experience creates a memory that we carry with us forever. These memories are our personal histories, stories we tell and the legacies we leave behind. They allow us to feel, to connect and to appreciate the richness of what life has to offer.

We find our greatest growth in challenging experiences. They force us to adapt, to learn and to become better versions of ourselves. Shared experiences create bonds and connections that bridge the gaps between individuals, communities and cultures. That's when you develop a mindset of community. Embrace every experience, learn from them, grow with them.

Life experiences, both positive and negative, can shape your mindset. Traumatic experiences can lead to a negative or fixed mindset while positive experiences can encourage a growth mindset. But if you are aware of what shapes the mindset, you can choose the right mindset. It all depends on how you perceive it.

Adversity & Challenges

Name a great person who hasn't faced adversity of a great magnitude. There are none. It's pretty hard to think of a truly great person who hasn't faced some significant challenges or adversity in their life. Now think about some of history's greatest figures.

Take someone like Nelson Mandela, for instance. He spent 27 years in prison for his fight against apartheid in South Africa. That's some serious adversity but it's also what helped shape him into the remarkable leader he became.

How about Mahatma Gandhi? He faced countless challenges and obstacles in his nonviolent struggle for India's independence from British rule. Those hardships only made his determination and greatness shine even brighter.

Even in the world of business and innovation, figures like Steve Jobs faced their fair share of setbacks and adversity. It's the way they dealt with those challenges that set them apart and made them great.

Greatness is forged in the fires of adversity. Greatness and adversity go hand in hand. It's the trials and tribulations that people overcome that truly define their greatness.

Life is a journey, destination is death. And the journey will be full of adversities. Adversity is a teacher. It teaches us life's most profound lessons. Adversity is like the crucible in which our character is forged. It tests our spirit, our endurance, our patience and the value of perseverance.

It is through adversity that we test our character with the ability to bounce back, to stand up again after falling and face the future with renewed determination. It's in the face of these challenges that we often discover our true strength and resilience.

Challenges stretch us beyond our comfort zones. They push us to acquire new skills and knowledge. When confronted with adversity, our minds become more creative, seeking innovative solutions to overcome obstacles.

Facing challenges and adversity can be a catalyst for developing resilience and a growth mindset. Overcoming obstacles leads to a sense of accomplishment and increased self-confidence. That's why people who have overcome adversities are our role models.

Lifelong Learning

"I have developed a habit of not knowing the people who know it all, yet the last book they read was in the classroom."

There's something special about people who keep on learning, who keep exploring new horizons and soaking up knowledge like a sponge. So, when I come across those who've let their intellectual curiosity stagnate, it's a bit of a head-scratcher, I'll admit. After all, life's a never-ending classroom and there's always something new to discover, don't you think?

In this fast-paced world where change is the only constant, the importance of lifelong learning cannot be overstated. It's a mindset and a commitment to continually seeking knowledge and growth throughout our lives.

For many, including myself, Learning is an inherently rewarding experience. Lifelong learning is a pathway to personal growth and self improvement. It allows us to explore our passions, develop new interests and unlock our full potential. It promotes a deeper understanding of the world. It enables us to be informed and wise.

Life is a journey of continuous discovery and growth. There is always something new worth learning about. It's an investment in yourself and your future. As the saying goes *"Once you stop learning, you start dying."*.

Exposure to new ideas, new concepts and new perspectives will definitely lead to a more open and adaptable mindset.

Role Models and Influences

You know, when I see people looking up to those social media sensations and treating them as role models, it leaves me a bit perplexed. I mean, when did influence, fame, money and power become the yardstick for who we should look up to? It's a head-scratcher, really.

Now, I'm not here to tell you how to live your life; that's entirely up to you. But imagine the positive impact it could have on the younger generation if they had some truly remarkable role models. Greatness, my friend, doesn't come cheap. It's not about the glitz and glamor; it's about the values, character and accomplishments that truly inspire. So, the choice is yours but I can't help but think that a world with more genuine role models would be a better place for everyone, especially our kids.

A role model is that shining example who inspires and motivates us to be our best selves. It's not just about admiring someone from afar; it's about learning from their actions and values and how we can apply those lessons to our own lives.

You see, role models come in many forms - they can be a parent, a teacher, a friend, a public figure or even a historical figure. But no matter who they are, the impact they have is undeniable. Role models show us what's possible. They inspire us to dream big, to set higher goals and to strive for excellence in our endeavors. They show us how to lead by example, to empower others and to make a positive impact in our communities and the world.

Just knowing that someone has been where we are and succeeded can be a tremendous source of encouragement. They have walked paths we're yet to traverse. Learning from their experiences can help us avoid pitfalls and make better decisions in our own journeys. Role models can provide that boost of confidence and belief in our own potential.

The people we surround ourselves with, including role models and mentors, can significantly impact our mindset. Positive role models can inspire a growth mindset, while negative influences can reinforce a fixed mindset.

CHAPTER FIVE

PHYSICAL

Femininity & Masculinity

If you don't protect what's yours, they will take away everything. By everything, I mean, everything.

First they destroyed culture. Now they are attacking families. Families have no more true autonomy. There are attempts to regulate families to a very fundamental level. Father won't be called father. Mother won't be called mother. They should be called "birthing people". There are attacks on self, the very nature of man and woman. Men are not men. Women are not women. There is no respect for families, there is no respect for the higher nature of man and woman. This is moral death.

Abraham Lincoln once asked an audience how many legs a dog has if you count the tail as a leg. When they answered "Five", Lincoln told them that the answer was "Four". The fact that you called the tail a leg did not make it a leg.

For now that's the problem in some societies but it will spread worldwide like a virus. For the confused, only tough times can test who is who. Only tough times can tell what a family really is. Until then the system will control it all. Be wise, How come external things influence and control your own identity and your family's identity. Beware of the twisting of the facts.

Let's talk about nature first, which is present in both men and women. Masculine and Feminine, the two extremes, can meet and blend and play with each other. The world as we know it owes its existence to the cooperative dance of the masculine and the feminine.

Masculine and feminine energies are not opposing forces in a battle for dominance; rather they are two essential halves of a harmonious whole. To deny the significance of either would be to undermine the very existence of yours. A harmonious coexistence is not a luxury; it is a necessity.

When we embrace both the masculine and feminine in their full glory, we unlock the boundless potential of our collective human experience. They are equally important, equally essential and neither can be truly appreciated in isolation.

Femininity

"We shall never know all the good that a simple smile can do." - Mother Teresa

In the gentle cadence of a mother's lullaby, femininity finds its voice, cradling the world in the soothing embrace of nurturing care. It is the silent strength of a woman who faces adversity with resilience, who carries burdens with a quiet dignity and who emerges from the storm with an unwavering grace that inspires us all.

Femininity's beauty resides in the unapologetic celebration of vulnerability and the freedom to express a wide spectrum of emotions. It is the courage to be authentic, to feel deeply and to share one's heart with the world.

The beauty of femininity lies in the depths of empathy, an intuitive understanding of the human heart that speaks in whispers, listens without judgment and offers solace in times of despair. It is the unspoken language of compassion that unites and heals the fractured fragments of our souls.

Masculinity

"Brave, bold men, these are what we want. What we want is vigour in the blood, strength in the nerves, iron muscles and nerves of steel, not softening namby-pamby ideas." - Swami Vivekananda

In the ancient epic of the Ramayana, we find a portrayal of masculinity that stands as a luminous example.

Rama's quest to save his beloved Sita, who was abducted by the demon king Ravana, serves as the testimony of masculine virtues. His strength, akin to a mountain, symbolizes the unyielding determination to overcome adversity. His dedication, a river flowing through his heart, reveals an unbreakable commitment to his partner.

Yet, it's not just physical might that defines Rama's masculinity. He demonstrates a profound respect for Sita, her choices and her integrity, treating her with the utmost honor and love. In doing so, he showcases a deeper facet of masculinity, the capacity for empathy and understanding.

Rama's journey is a testament to the notion that masculinity isn't merely about power but about using that power for protection, support and the well being of those cherished.

On the other hand, Ravana is a formidable warrior with ten heads and vast knowledge, symbolizing physical, intellectual and spiritual prowess. His audacious abduction of Sita showcases a sense of authority and entitlement.

His inability to respect boundaries, especially concerning Sita, are aspects of masculinity that can lead to negative consequences. His hubris and arrogance ultimately lead to his downfall, illustrating the dangers of unchecked masculinity.

Ravana's character serves as a reminder that masculinity, when distorted or unchecked, can lead to destructive consequences.

Masculinity is about being responsible and strong for the people you care about. It's like a powerful shield against life's storms and a mighty sword of determination to carve pathways through adversity to protect and provide for your loved ones. Being strong and dependable is honorable.

Holistic Fitness

Healthy Life & Self Defense

You should look at fitness holistically from the perspective of healthy living and from the perspective of self defense.

Let's talk fitness in the context of self defense. In a long life everyone faces physical threats and adversity and our future generations will face the same. Self defense is not about seeking confrontation but being ready to protect yourself in a dangerous world. It's about being prepared and capable of protecting yourself when the need arises. Being fit means you have the physical strength and power to strike, grapple or immobilize an opponent. Whether it's a punch, kick or a hold, having strong muscles can make a significant difference in your ability to fend off an attacker.

Situations can be intense and may require you to exert yourself for an extended period. Good level of your cardio fitness ensures you can keep up the fight or escape if necessary. You don't want to tire out too quickly when your safety is on the line. Being agile and quick on your feet can help you avoid dangerous situations or evade an attacker. Quick reflexes can mean the difference between getting away unscathed or being overpowered.

Natural disasters and wars involve prolonged periods of physical exertion, whether it's evacuating from a disaster zone, carrying heavy gear in a combat situation or helping others in need. Good endurance and stamina can make a significant difference in your ability to endure these challenges. In war strength is vital for carrying equipment and weapons. Being physically strong can help you overcome obstacles like moving debris, clearing the paths. In emergencies you may need to carry essential supplies like food, water and medical equipment which can be heavy. You may have to go through different challenges like climbing, swimming or crawling. A fit body recovers more quickly. This can be a critical factor in survival during disasters or conflicts.

Bullies often pick on those they perceive as vulnerable. Physical fitness can change that perception. When you look and feel strong, bullies may think twice before trying to intimidate you. Nobody wants to mess with a person who can inflict greater damage. When you feel good about your body and abilities, you're less likely to be an easy target for bullies. Confidence can act as a deterrent and make bullies think twice before targeting you.

Physical Fitness is about being better prepared to face the physical and mental demands of these extreme situations. Being fit can boost your self confidence. Knowing that you're in good shape and can handle physical confrontations and natural disasters.

Now let's talk fitness in the context of healthy living. It's not a one-size-fits-all concept and it doesn't have to involve extreme workouts. It's about finding what works for you and making it a part of your daily routine.

Being fit improves your quality of life. You can engage in various activities, hobbies and adventures without physical limitations. Whether it's hiking, playing sports or just running around with your kids, only fit people can do it effectively after a certain age. Regular cardio, strength training and flexibility workouts contribute to better physical health. It helps maintain a healthy weight, lowers the risk of chronic diseases like diabetes and improves overall bodily functions.

Fitness isn't just about the body, it's a boon for the mind too. Exercise releases endorphins, the "feel-good" hormones, which can reduce stress, anxiety and depression. It's a natural mood booster and can enhance your mental well-being. When you're fit you have more energy and vitality to tackle daily tasks and enjoy life to the fullest. You don't get tired as quickly and you're better equipped to take on challenges.

Train For War

"When the time comes some will hide and cry, some will march forward and fight."

There is no peace time, only preparation time and war time. It is impossible to go through life without fights and wars. When the time comes some will hide and cry, some will march forward and fight.

Sharpen Your Sword, Daily.

Training like a warrior is not a mere physical endeavor; it's a holistic transformation of mind, body and spirit. It begins with a sacred commitment, an unwavering vow to become the best version of oneself. A warrior's journey starts with mental discipline. Cultivate unwavering focus and a resilient spirit that can weather any storm.

Train your body as if it were your most valuable weapon. Adopt a well-rounded fitness regimen, incorporating strength, agility and endurance. Fuel your body with the right nutrition, akin to a warrior's diet. Consume lean protein, whole grains and an abundance of fresh fruits and vegetables. Hydration is important consider it your lifeblood.

Just as battles have periods of respite, warriors must rest. Sleep is your body's reset button; cherish it. Proper recovery ensures peak performance when it's time to train or fight. Never give up, a warrior never quits. Even in the face of seemingly insurmountable odds, persevere. The path to becoming a true warrior is a long and arduous one but the rewards are immeasurable.

Learn martial arts or combat techniques to build both combat skills and physical discipline.

Form bonds with fellow trainees; they are your allies, your comrades. In their support, you will find strength.

By following this path you are not only building physical strength; You are forging an disciplined mind and an indomitable spirit.

Fitness and Sports

When my wife and I first moved to Bengaluru, we did something a bit unconventional. Instead of splurging on sofas and fancy furniture for our new place, we decided to set up a small gym. Yeah, it might sound a bit odd but we took the budget we had for furniture and invested it in a few weights and workout machines. That gym setup is still with us to this day. Now we have added a few outdoor cycles also.

Now, I won't deny that we can be a bit on the lazy side but that's beside the point. What I'm getting at here is the importance of having our priorities straight. We realized that our health and fitness were a top priority for us, so we made that investment instead of going for the typical home furnishings. It's all about what matters most to you and for us staying active and healthy came first.

The reason people don't play sports is that we are getting lonely day by day. We are getting busy day by day. Even if we have 30 minutes free, we'll fill it with more work and social media distractions. If you have 30 minutes free, keep it free. That's important. That's how you make time for what's important. If fitness is important, you will make time for that, but only if you learn to be free. If you want to build an athletic body you must run, cycle, swim or play sports.

Few years ago I bought a folding bike for myself and a few other bikes for kids of their choice. And it's one of the best decisions I made. I love cycling early in the morning, it's a holistic fitness activity that benefits my heart, muscles and mind. When you pedal away, you're giving your heart a workout. Cycling is an excellent cardiovascular exercise that gets the blood pumping, strengthens your heart and improves circulation. The wind in your hair, the open road and the rhythmic motion of pedaling all contribute to reducing stress and boosting your mood. As your heart rate increases during cycling, your lungs work harder, too. This can improve lung function over time. Cycling helps build endurance. Whether you're going for a short sprint or a long-distance ride, you'll find yourself gradually building up your stamina. If you're looking to shed some weight, cycling is your friend. It burns calories and you can cover a lot of ground. Most importantly it keeps me in connection with the smiling faces, kids.

Sports is a team game and it not only keeps us fit but we also make friends, build bonds and enjoy the sport. When you're out there on the field or court, you're moving, running and giving your heart a workout. All that action gets your heart pumping, improving your cardiovascular health and endurance. Whether you're dribbling a basketball or swimming laps, your muscles are getting a fantastic workout. This not only builds strength but also helps to tone your body. You're twisting, turning and reaching, which improves your flexibility and coordination. It makes your body more agile and less prone to injuries. Staying active in sports helps you manage your weight. All that running and jumping burns calories, helping to keep those extra pounds at bay. If you can keep yourself free and stay close to few friends, then this is one of the best thing you can do for your fitness.

Healthy Living

Living a healthy life nowadays can be quite the challenge. Cities are covered in pollution and fast food joints are on every corner. Finding fresh, wholesome vegetables sometimes feels like searching for a needle in a haystack. And let's not forget the struggle of finding a big, natural green space nearby for a refreshing morning or evening walk. It's a tough situation, no doubt.

But you know what? Despite all these obstacles, there are inspiring examples of change that remind us that it's still possible if we truly desire it. There are people out there making a difference and their stories can be the spark that ignites hope and motivation. Here is an example from my journal which I use as a tool of my artistic expression.

The Beauty of Bengaluru
A Lake, An Island, A Castle, A Rainbow
May 3, 2023 #Journal

For a decade I have called Bengaluru my home and within a mere walking distance from my home rests an 80 acre lake with a tapu inside - The Agara Lake.

For years this lake was left to suffer the consequences of neglect and pollution, a stark reflection of a society preoccupied with urban growth. However, in 2018, With a grant of 16 crore, Karnataka Lake Conservation Authorities set about rejuvenating this once forgotten lake.

Today as I strolled along the lake with my family we were treated to a magnificent display of nature's beauty. As the rain poured down, a magnificent rainbow arced across the sky, forming a perfect backdrop to the lake, the island and the castle-like building.

I could not resist the urge to capture this moment of sublime tranquility, a snapshot of the transformation that the Agara Lake has undergone.

At the center of the lake sits a small island adorned with lush greenery that serves as a serene oasis of calm amidst the bustling city life, main attraction for birds.

The jogging and cycling lanes encircle the lake stretch for a vast distance of 3 kilometers providing a place for individuals to escape from the stress of everyday life.

Benches are placed around the lake's perimeter, a space to sit and luxuriate in the gentle breeze while admiring the awe inspiring view.

Along these lanes are outdoor gyms allowing people to engage in workout while relishing the breathtaking surroundings and a playground to provide a delightful space for kids to frolic and play.

And for avid bird watchers Agara Lake is a veritable paradise, home to an abundance of feathered creatures that soar through the skies above.

Agara Lake is a precious jewel in the heart of Silicon Valley, a blessing for the residents and an inspiring story of transformation. It's The Beauty of Bengaluru.

Photograph available @ MukeshDaily on Instagram.

Life is too magnificent to be lived in the shadows of lethargy when it can be experienced with the radiant glow of health. It is a rebellion against the chains of inactivity. It's the invitation to unlock the potential of the body, you become the athlete of your own life, the champion of your health.

In every dawn that breaks and every sunset that graces our existence, lies a chance to not only safeguard our health but to revel in the exquisite joy of self care. So embrace this call to action. Dedicate the moments that life grants you to fortify and celebrate the temple of your own being - your body. The path to a healthier, happier life is within your grasp if you don't waste the valuable time.

Illness is an unwelcome visitor that often knocks on our doors. It is true some illness may strike despite our best efforts. Throughout history it's a persistent truth in the human experience. However, let us not overlook the impact our choices can have on its occurrence. Each day presents an opportunity, a canvas upon which we can paint a healthier and vibrant life.

Diet & Nutritions

More than One billion people worldwide suffer from protein deficiency.

The path to a healthier, happier and more vibrant future begins on our plates.

In a world where fast food chains seem to outnumber the stars in the sky and where sugary beverages flow more freely than fresh water, the need for a healthy diet has never been more pressing. The call for a shift toward nutritious, balanced eating is not just a suggestion; it is an imperative for our well-being, longevity and the vitality of our future generations.

More than One billion people worldwide suffer from protein deficiency. Protein is important because it provides the amino acids your body needs to build and repair muscle. Protein is the building block of muscle tissue. When you work out, you create tiny tears in your muscles and protein is essential for repairing and rebuilding them. This process is what makes your muscles grow and get stronger.

Protein can help with weight management. It's more satiating than carbohydrates or fats, meaning it can help control your appetite and reduce calorie intake, which is important if you're looking to shed some extra pounds. When you're on a calorie-restricted diet, your body can start breaking down muscle tissue for energy. Adequate protein intake can help preserve your lean body mass and ensure that the weight you lose is primarily fat.

Protein isn't just about muscles; it's essential for repairing and growing all kinds of body tissues, including skin, hair and nails. This contributes to an overall healthy and fit appearance. You must think about this, do you have enough protein.

Action item: *Do a holistic research on what is your current protein intake and how much protein you need per kg body weight.*

Consider for a moment the repercussions of poor dietary choices. Obesity, heart disease, diabetes and a host of other chronic ailments plague millions of lives. The consequences ripple through families, communities and healthcare systems. The toll on our physical and mental health is undeniable.

When we make mindful choices about what we eat, we exercise control over our own well-being. A diet rich in whole grains, fruits, vegetables, proteins and essential nutrients provides our bodies with the fuel they need to thrive. Energy levels soar and physical vitality is restored. Nutrient dense foods are our first line of defense against chronic diseases. They bolster our immune systems, reduce the risk of most diseases and help manage conditions like diabetes and hypertension.

What we eat not only affects our bodies but also our brain. A balanced diet can sharpen cognitive functions, boost memory and promote holistic well being.

CHAPTER SIX

INTELLECTUAL

Knowledge & Wisdom

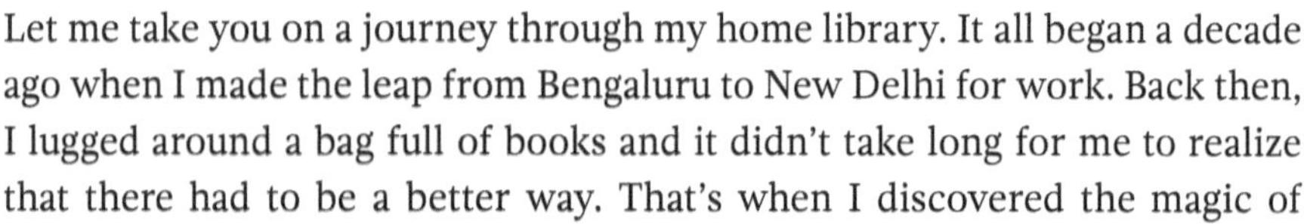

Let me take you on a journey through my home library. It all began a decade ago when I made the leap from Bengaluru to New Delhi for work. Back then, I lugged around a bag full of books and it didn't take long for me to realize that there had to be a better way. That's when I discovered the magic of Kindle and for a good chunk of time I was engrossed in hundreds of books on that electronic digital device.

But life has a way of changing, doesn't it? As I settled in one place with my family, I felt this growing need for something more tangible - A Home Library. You see, having a library at home can transform your entire environment. While a Kindle might sit quietly in a corner, a library filled with physical books is impossible to ignore. It's like a silent invitation whispering to you to dive into its pages and soon enough you find yourself heeding the call. A library wields a unique and powerful influence.

Today, I have a library filled with hundreds of books spanning a multitude of domains. It's not just about self help or any single genre; my collection spans literature, philosophy, economics, history, politics, spirituality, health, creativity, nature, wildlife, engineering, innovation, business and the list goes on. The beauty of it is that my kids have also fallen in love with the world of books, each finding their own treasures to explore. And when friends come over, they can't help but be drawn to the library's allure, many times leaving with borrowed books in hand. That, My friend, is the magic of a home library. I think it sets the culture of learning at my home.

You know, these days, it's becoming increasingly rare to find a home with a proper library. It's all about those big TVs and the ever enticing world of social media. Just take a moment to reflect on that for a second.

Imagine a world where curiosity slumbers, where questions go unasked and where the thirst for knowledge remains unquenched. In such a world, intellectual pursuits are dormant and the mind like a garden untended, withers. But in the realm of intellectual exploration, the spirit awakens, the mind flourishes and the horizons of understanding expand.

An intellectual pursuit is an invitation to unravel the mysteries of the universe, to probe the depths of the human psyche and to traverse the corridors of history and culture. It is the sanctuary where ignorance is dispelled, where myths are debunked and where truths are unveiled.

"If the only tool you have is a hammer, you tend to see every problem as a nail." - Abraham Maslow

Let's Talk About Stock Markets For A Moment.

It's a well known fact that 9 out of 10 people in the stock market end up losing money. Many people also fall victim to financial frauds and scams, leaving them with empty pockets. So, why does that happen? Well, it's a complex issue and there's more to it than meets the eye.

There's a saying in Hindi that goes, "Most people have a thought of one and a half meters." In other words, their perspective is limited. One of the key reasons behind this trend is that many people lack a broad understanding of various subjects like economics, history, psychology. Their knowledge base is narrow and they often can't see the bigger picture, including the historical, social and economic aspects of things.

When you dive into the world of stocks or financial investments without a well-rounded understanding, it's like navigating a complex maze blindfolded. So broadening your knowledge and looking at the broader context can be your shield against potential losses and scams in the financial world. In the complex game of finance, having a wider perspective can make all the difference.

Understanding economics gives you the tools to make informed decisions in your personal and professional life. It helps you comprehend how the world works, why prices rise and fall and how policies impact our wallets. With some basic economic knowledge you can navigate your finances more effectively, whether it's budgeting, investing or planning for the future.

Economics is also important for understanding societal issues. It helps us grasp concepts like poverty, inequality and unemployment. When you learn about economics, you can engage in informed discussions and even advocate for policies that promote a fair and prosperous society.

History isn't just about ancient events or dusty old books; it's a treasure trove of lessons that can help us navigate the complex world of money. The past holds valuable insights into how economies, markets and financial systems have behaved. What worked and what didn't. What was scams and what wasn't. Scams and frauds aren't new. By studying historical trends we can better understand the causes and effects of financial crises, market booms and busts. Historical knowledge helps us recognize patterns and avoid repeating past mistakes.

Our minds play a significant role in how we approach financial matters. It's not just about numbers and charts; it's about understanding our own human nature and how it influences the choices we make with our money. Emotions like fear, greed and overconfidence can lead us to make impulsive decisions that may not be in our best interest. The fear of losing money can make us overly conservative, missing out on potential opportunities for growth. On the flip side, excessive greed can lead us to take unnecessary risks. By recognizing these psychological factors we can make more rational and informed financial decisions.

The crux of my argument is that to avoid being deceived, it's essential to possess a comprehensive grasp of various facets of life and societies.

World will fool you, it's your job to be wise. Knowledge is not wisdom, Applied knowledge is. A lot of people know a lot about the stock market but they lose money. A lot of people know a lot about health but they are not fit. Applied knowledge is wisdom, My Friend.

Action Item: *Do your holistic research on stock markets, money, financial scams and frauds.*

Let's Talk About Medicines & Vaccines For A Moment.

Let's talk about the impact of medicines and vaccines on our health, especially in the context of a pandemic. We all have gone through Covid 19. Every year there are many small instances of deadly virus spread but they are contained in a short geography. Covid 19 was a pandemic, a situation where a deadly virus was spreading worldwide like wildfire and billions of lives were at risk. Now, you've got a vaccine that can prevent this catastrophe but it's not without its flaws. There's a chance that a few thousand people might experience serious side effects and unfortunately some might even lose their lives.

It's a real tough call, isn't it? This is the kind of decision governments often have to grapple with. They're in the unenviable position of having to make choices that in theory may sound immoral. Saving the masses at the potential cost of a few individuals is a heavy burden to bear. That's the only practical choice. They have to weigh the greater good against the potential harm. It's a complex and difficult decision to make and it's one that carries a heavy moral and ethical weight.

It's about the tough choices that leaders must make to protect public health. Government is responsible for collective public health. You are responsible for yours.

Not all medicines work the same way for everyone. Our bodies are unique and our responses to medications can vary. They can be a lifeline but they also require caution and informed choices. That's why medication is always taken after a doctor's consultation and not directly from a medical store. Doctors can weigh the benefits against the risks. There are definitely consequences of medication. Sometimes the very remedy that's supposed to make us better can have bigger consequences.

Protecting yourself is your responsibility. Nobody can think about you or your conditions and your situations. Be wise, My Friend.

__Action Item__ : Do your holistic research on Covid 19 vaccines and It's positive and negative Impacts.

Let's Talk About Food & Nutritions For A Moment.

Science has shown that the food we consume can even affect our hormones – those chemical messengers that regulate so many bodily functions. The food we choose to eat has a profound influence on our overall well-being. It's not just about filling our stomachs; it's about nourishing our bodies and minds.

Now, before you go and make any major dietary changes, it's important to exercise a healthy dose of caution. You see, science is an ever-evolving field. We're constantly learning new things and not everything is set in stone. Research can sometimes be influenced by various biases and that's why it's always a good idea to do your own homework.

When it comes to what you put in your body, don't just jump on the latest diet or nutrition trend without a second thought. It's wise to have a healthy skepticism and carefully consider the potential impacts on your body. After all, your health is at stake and it's worth taking the time to make informed decisions. So, in a world where information is constantly changing and evolving, make sure you're your own best advocate when it comes to what you eat.

Think about Fast food, loaded with excess calories, unhealthy fats and sugar. It is one of the leading sources of health problems from weight gain, obesity and a host of related health issues including heart disease and diabetes. Point is only you can care about your health, everybody else cares about their profit. Government cares about its economy.

Science doesn't have all the answers. Corporates don't care about your health, they care enough to be legal, after that it's all profit. Be wise, My Friend.

Action Item: *Do your holistic research on Soybean and its impact on hormones.*

Life is like a grand puzzle with many pieces. Having a broad knowledge isn't about being a know-it-all; it's about having the right puzzle pieces to make sense of the world around you. It's like having a bunch of tools in your toolbox. The right tool you have, more effectively you can tackle life's challenges. A broader understanding of different perspectives and experiences helps you relate to people from all walks of life. Whether it's understanding different cultures, solving problems or making informed decisions that extensive knowledge about different fields comes in handy.

In the pursuit of wisdom, you become a disciple of the vast library of human thought. You embark on a quest to plumb the fathoms of philosophy, to traverse the galaxies of literature and to dissect the wonders of science. You stand on the shoulders of giants who have bequeathed their insights, their discoveries and their wisdom, each text, each equation and each idea a torch to light your way.

It is an exercise in critical thinking, in disciplined analysis and in the cultivation of intellectual acumen. It is an affirmation that you are the captain of your own intellect, the author of your own intellectual narrative and the guardian of the legacy of knowledge.

So, why should you have an intellectual pursuit? Because life is too intricate to be perceived in monochrome. Because your mind yearns for the challenges only it can overcome, the questions only it can answer and the intellectual adventures only it can undertake.

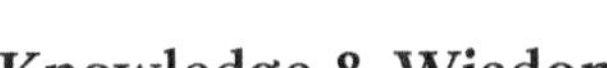

Knowledge & Wisdom

"Specialization is for insects." - Robert Heinlein

Deep within our hearts, a powerful yearning beckons us toward the uncharted territories of learning, exploration and the pursuit of new knowledge and experiences. The very essence of our being thrives on the thrill of discovery and the joy of expanding our horizons. It's an innate longing that fuels our intellectual and emotional growth, fostering a sense of fulfillment and purpose in our lives.

Prioritize intellectual engagement, for it is through knowledge and understanding that we truly unlock our potential to make the world a better place. It's a compelling necessity for personal growth and societal progress. Intellectuals have the power to shape individuals into informed, critical thinkers and to drive positive change in the world.

Curiosity

The journey begins with an insatiable curiosity. Develop a hunger for knowledge and an eagerness to explore a wide array of subjects. Question everything and seek to understand the deeper layers of the world around you.

Recognize that learning is a lifelong endeavor. Commit to ongoing self-improvement. The foundation of lifelong learning is curiosity. Cultivate a thirst for knowledge, ask questions and maintain a childlike wonder about the world around you.

Approach new ideas and experiences with an open mind. Embrace the unknown, challenge your preconceptions and be willing to change your perspective.

Critical Thinking

You know, it's really quite baffling how some people seem to put their brains in the refrigerator and then go ahead believing just about anything and doing some pretty darn stupid things in this world. I mean, it's like they've taken a vacation from common sense! But hey, we've all had our moments of lapses in judgment, right? It's just a good reminder for the rest of us to keep our thinking caps on and make wise decisions.

Challenge your own beliefs and ideas. Critical thinking involves questioning assumptions and examining concepts from multiple perspectives. It's a tool to help you develop a deeper and more well-rounded understanding of any topic.

Critical thinking is not a luxury of intellectuals but a necessity in our information rich, fast paced world. It's our ability to solve problems, make informed choices and truly understand the world around us. So, I encourage you to embrace the power of critical thinking, to question, to analyze and to seek deeper understanding. It's a skill that will serve you well in every facet of life.

In a world overwhelmed with information, critical thinking helps us discern the reliable from the unreliable. It allows us to make informed decisions, separating fact from fiction and avoiding pitfalls. Critical thinking allows us to see issues from multiple angles. It is critical thinking that allows us to question the status quo, challenge assumptions and envision novel solutions. It encourages us to assess our beliefs, biases and preconceptions. There is no self awareness without critical thinking.

Experience the World

"Books can only reveal what is already in your experience."

Travel, explore different cultures and immerse yourself in new experiences. This can provide fresh perspectives and insights.

Immerse yourself into different cultures. It's an opportunity to appreciate the customs, traditions and histories that make each society unique. Travel and exploration open our minds to new perspectives. It challenges our preconceptions, fosters empathy and helps us understand the world through the eyes of others. It broadens our perspectives. We can now consider what we might not have considered earlier. When you return from a trip, you can bring some books from that culture. Why not?

Read Widely

"The more that you read, the more things you will know. The more that you learn, the more places you'll go." - Dr. Seuss

Reading is the cornerstone of intellectual growth. Read books, articles and texts from various fields and genres. Diversify your reading list to include literature, science, history, philosophy and more. Break down the barriers between different fields of knowledge. Explore how ideas from one area can inform or enrich another. This can lead to innovative insights and a holistic understanding of complex issues.

Reading is a window to the world and when we read widely, we open countless windows, allowing a flood of knowledge and perspective to enter our lives. When we dive into the pages of different kinds of books, we step into the shoes of different characters and authors. We encounter differing viewpoints and we learn to evaluate and form our own opinions.

Reading widely exposes us to a variety of topics, cultures and experiences. It broadens our horizons, giving us a more comprehensive view of the world. A well-read person is often a better communicator. Reading widely enriches our vocabulary and helps us articulate thoughts and ideas more effectively.

So why not pick up books on subjects you've never considered, dive into genres you've never explored and journey into the uncharted territories of knowledge.

Study the Classics

"A classic is a book that has never finished saying what it has to say." - Italo Calvino

Explore the timeless works of literature, philosophy and science. These texts have shaped the foundations of human thought and offer profound insights into the human condition.

The classics have stood the test of time for a reason. They contain universal themes and timeless wisdom that continue to resonate with people of all ages and cultures. They explore profound themes and moral dilemmas. They invite us to reflect on the human condition, our values and our place in the world.

Classics provide us with a deep understanding of the cultures and societies from which they originated. They offer a window into the past and a mirror to the present. When we study the classics we connect with the historical context in which they were written. This connection can deepen our understanding of the past.

Many classic works are celebrated for their exceptional writing and storytelling. They set the bar high for literary craftsmanship and reading them can be a lesson in language and narrative artistry. They've influenced countless works of literature, film and art.

Practice Mindfulness

Intellectual growth is not just about external knowledge but also internal self awareness. Engage in mindfulness practices, such as meditation, to understand your thought processes and foster deeper introspection.

In a world filled with distractions, mindfulness helps us hone our focus. It trains our minds to concentrate on the task at hand, enhancing productivity and effectiveness. Mindfulness empowers us to recognize and control our emotions. It allows us to respond thoughtfully rather than react impulsively, improving our decision making.

By being present with our thoughts and feelings, mindfulness leads to self awareness. It allows us to understand our values, desires and aspirations. It's about savoring the small moments, finding peace in the chaos and nurturing a deeper connection with ourselves and the world around us.

Discussion and Debate

We hold so many false beliefs and it's hard to question what we believe to be true. Sometimes, all it takes is a different perspective or a simple question from a friend and suddenly we start to see things in a whole new light. It's like a little wake up call for our mind and that, my friend, is pretty darn great.

Engage in meaningful conversations with others. Debate ideas, share perspectives and learn from different viewpoints. Surrounding yourself with diverse thinkers can expand your intellectual horizons.

Through discussion and debate, we learn. We expose ourselves to new ideas, information and insights that challenge our preconceptions and foster personal and intellectual growth.

In a world with differing opinions and beliefs, the ability to discuss and debate is important for conflict resolution. It's a peaceful avenue for addressing disagreements and finding common ground. Debate and brainstorming can stimulate innovation and creative problem solving. It allows us to question the status quo and envision novel solutions to complex issues.

In our democratic societies debate is the way of civic engagement. Debate is how you participate in political processes and hold those in power accountable. Debate is not just a matter of expressing opinions but a means to deeper understanding, progress and change.

Write and Reflect

It's pretty incredible to think that just a year ago, I decided to start journaling and here I am today, writing this book. It's one of those moments when you realize that, somewhere down the line, all those little dots you've been connecting in your life start to make sense. So, here I am, putting pen to paper and turning my thoughts into something more profound. It's all about the journey, isn't it?

Writing helps clarify your thoughts and synthesize what you've learned. Keep a journal, write essays or start a blog to document your intellectual journey and share your insights with others.

Whether through journaling, essays, poetry or simply taking time to ponder life's experiences, writing offers a means to record our thoughts, understand and express ourselves. Writing provides a creative outlet for self expression. It allows us to communicate our feelings, desires and experiences, even when spoken words may fail us. Journaling serves as a record of our journey. It allows us to look back and see how far we've come, making it a valuable source of motivation and growth.

Writing forces us to organize our thoughts and ideas. It's a process of distilling the chaos of our minds into coherent, structured narratives. This clarity extends to our thinking and decision making. When we write we sometimes find solutions to problems we've been grappling with.

To reflect is to look inward, to pause and ponder the experiences and thoughts that shape our lives. It's a fundamental tool for self-awareness. Through reflection, we learn from our experiences. It's a means of extracting wisdom from our past, allowing us to grow and make more informed choices in the future. When we reflect we can analyze challenges and setbacks, seeking solutions and lessons that might have otherwise gone unnoticed.

CHAPTER SEVEN

CREATIVE

Expressions & Creation

Picture a world where the canvas remains blank, where the song remains unsung and where the unwritten story lingers in the shadows. A world devoid of creative pursuits is like a symphony without melody, a garden without flowers and a heart without a song.

It is the sanctuary where the mind finds solace, where the heart finds its voice and where the spirit soars to new heights. It is in the act of creation that we glimpse the infinite potential that resides within us, waiting to be unleashed.

Engaging in a creative pursuit is an act of rebellion against conformity, a revolt against mediocrity and a declaration that you will not be a passive observer of life. It is an embrace of the unique, a celebration of the authentic and a declaration that your voice, your vision and your story matter. It is an assertion that you are the author of your narrative, the painter of your canvas and the composer of your melody.

In the world of creative pursuits, you are invited to break the rules, color outside the lines and dream beyond the confines of reality. It is a pursuit where mistakes become masterpieces, imperfections become beauty and failures become stepping stones to success. It is a tribute to the audacity of the human spirit, which refuses to be shackled by the mundane and the ordinary.

So, why should you have a creative pursuit? Because life is too extraordinary to be lived in grayscale when it can be painted in vibrant hues.

Because your soul yearns for the music only you can compose, the stories only you can tell and the art only you can create. Because a creative pursuit is not a pastime; it is a lifeline to the core of your being, a journey of self-discovery and a boundless wellspring of joy.

In the act of creation, you become the artist of your own existence, the maestro of your own symphony and the author of your own story. And as you breathe life into your creative pursuit, you breathe life into your own spirit, infusing every day with the vibrancy of your unique expression. You become both the artist and the art, the creator and the creation.

Expressions & Creation

Creative expression serves as a mirror to the soul. It is an invitation to imagine, to dream, to connect and to understand. It reveals what words alone cannot convey, offering a profound glimpse into the artist's inner world, their dreams, fears, desires and unique perspective on life. It is what makes us human - art, literature, music and performance that reflects the evolution of our society and the essence of the human experience.

Emotions find their voice through creative expression. Whether it's the burst of colors on a canvas, the melodic cadence of a song or the passionate verses of a poem. It's a universal language, transcending cultural, linguistic and geographical barriers. It connects people on a deep level, conveying shared experiences and emotions, even when the artist and the audience are worlds apart. For many, creative expression serves as a form of healing. It provides a means to release emotional baggage, confront pain and find solace in the act of creation.

We all have those moments when we crack a joke and suddenly everyone's laughing and the atmosphere just becomes so much more pleasant. Humor is a wonderful tool for self expression available to everyone. Humor can break the ice, lighten the mood and even make the most boring topics entertaining.

Art is a profound form of human expression, a medium that enables us to convey complex emotions, ideas and stories. It serves as a mirror reflecting the diverse facets of our culture, society and individual experiences. Art has the power to inspire and evoke awe. Whether through the brilliance of a painting, the magic of a melody or the eloquence of a story, it invites us to see the world with fresh eyes and marvel at the wonder of human creativity.

Storytelling is the timeless art of conveying human experiences, knowledge and emotions through narrative. Whether shared around a campfire, written in books or transmitted through digital media, stories are what connects us. They transcend cultural and temporal boundaries, continuing to captivate and inspire individuals across generations and they serve as a bridge connecting the past to the present and future.

Photography

Photography, for me, is a way of creative expression. It's not a means to earn a living and I don't pursue it for the sole purpose of making money. Sometimes we need to step aside from the concept of turning every passion into a profession. It's not about chasing dollars; it's about following your heart. For me, photography is a cherished hobby, not a career. It's about capturing the essence of moments, freezing time and letting my imagination roam freely through the lens. You see, not everything in life is about monetary gains. Some pursuits are purely driven by love and passion.

Five years ago, I made a purchase that altered my perspective on photography entirely. I got myself a Canon M50 camera and I can tell you it was love at first sight. You see, it's not just about taking pictures, something you can effortlessly do with your smartphone. The real magic happens when you snap your first shot with a dedicated camera.

I've experimented with some of the best mobile phones on the market but let me tell you, there's no comparison. A dedicated camera, like the Canon M50, delivers an image quality and control that smartphones can only dream of. It's like comparing apples to oranges.

Now, don't get me wrong; I'm not in this for the money. I've invested a substantial amount of time and money in learning the craft and acquiring the right equipment. Over the years, I've added more prime lenses to my arsenal to cater to different purposes. There's the Sigma 16mm, perfect for those wide-angle shots, the Sigma 30mm for more standard shooting and the Canon 55-200mm to capture distant subjects.

This journey has been a labor of love, a passionate pursuit of the art of photography. It's not about making a quick buck; it's about capturing the world in ways that only a dedicated camera can. So, my Canon M50 and my growing collection of lenses are more than just tools – they're the gateway to a world of visual storytelling and artistic expression.

You can delve into the world of professional level photography simply because it brings you joy. There's a profound satisfaction in creating stunning photographs that goes beyond the scope of making a living. These are the pursuits that feed your soul, ignite your joy and offer genuine satisfaction. That, My friend, is what it means to truly live life.

Whether it's capturing portraits, candid moments, the beauty of nature, the fleeting scenes of the streets, I find myself deeply in love with it all. I immerse myself in the work of great photographers, I watch their videos, I devour their books and most importantly I enjoy every moment I spend with my camera, capturing moments through the lens. It's a passion for me.

Almost a year ago along with photography I started to journal. I started journaling what I experience when taking a photograph and here is one of the stories from my journal and as you read you can imagine the photograph, now if you like you can go and see the photograph on my instagram profile @ MukeshDaily. But first I want you to read.

Candid Photography For Parents

April 12, 2023 #Journal

As the setting sun dipped below the horizon, painting the sky in a breathtaking palette of orange and golden hues, I found myself in awe of the picturesque landscape before me.

Rows upon rows of golden wheat swayed gently in the evening breeze. And there, amidst the rustic beauty, was my son and baby nephew, who always roam around freely with a stick in one hand and a dinosaur in the other.

With my camera in hand, I stealthily captured the candid moments, innocent joy shining through each click of the shutter. Their carefree laughter was echoing through the fields as they ran and played.

Every candid shot tells a story of love, discovery and the magic of childhood. This was a story from Jan 10th, I hold onto these photographs in my heart to relive again.

Photograph available @ MukeshDaily on Instagram.

The point I am trying to make is that life is not about work, money and others. Life is much more than that. Where is your creative expression, give it a chance.

Photography is the art of capturing moments, emotions and stories through the lens of a camera. It freezes time, encapsulating the world in still frames that transcend the fleeting present. It captures the beauty of a single moment or the complexity of an entire lifetime. Each photograph tells a story, whether it's the quiet elegance of a landscape, the candid emotions of a portrait or the intricate details of an everyday scene. The power of a single photograph to convey emotion, tell stories and document history is profound.

Filmmaking

Let me take you back to the wild ride that was 2020. The COVID pandemic was just starting to rear its ugly head and at the same time, my little bundle of joy came into this world - my son was born! It was a crazy, tumultuous time and I found myself stuck in Bengaluru for the first few months, navigating this new chapter of my life.

But you know what? Every cloud has a silver lining and in my case, it was the chance to be with my baby boy. Let me tell you, there's nothing quite like it. Those adorable little faces, the pure and natural expressions of a baby and that incredible innocence that's beyond words, it's a feeling that's indescribable.

Now, during this unforgettable period, something remarkable happened. I decided to try my hand at filmmaking. I mean, what better way to capture these precious moments, right? I already had a camera and I went all in and invested in a few prime lenses and a professional filmmaking gimbal and you can't imagine that it opened up a whole new world for me.

Of course, I had to learn filmmaking, it wasn't all smooth sailing from the get go. But let me tell you, every moment I spent learning and practicing was worth it. I managed to capture some of the most priceless moments of my life, moments that my family and I will treasure forever.

"You can't record your today tomorrow even if you want to."

And that's precisely how I view filmmaking.

Kids, they grow up in the blink of an eye. One moment they're these tiny, adorable bundles of joy and the next, they're off to explore the world. It's so darn fast! But with filmmaking, I found a way to freeze those fleeting moments, to create a beautiful film of our lives. And it's not about money or fame, it's deeply personal.

I want to have those memories to hold onto to relive those precious moments over and over again. So, why not capture your life's story on film? It's a way of preserving the magic, the love and the sheer joy that life brings.

Filmmaking is the art of storytelling through motion and sound. It's a symphony of visual elements, dialogue, music and silence, orchestrated to convey a narrative that engages the senses and the emotions. Filmmakers are modern-day storytellers, weaving tales that transcend boundaries, cultures and languages.

Writing & Journaling

So, let me tell you about the day I first started journaling. It ranks right up there with my passion for photography and filmmaking as one of the best decisions I've ever made. Journaling is all about unleashing your inner artist and weaving stories from the threads of your life. And the beautiful thing is, no matter how trivial or grand, each entry in that journal is uniquely yours. It's your story, your narrative, your experience of the world. Here I share few pages when I first started journaling:

Picking Up A New Hobby - Journaling
April 10, 2023 #Journal

As I sit down with a digital pen in hand, I feel the surge of excitement course through me. I've decided to pick up a new hobby, a simple and profound idea to document my life - Journaling.

I have been documenting my life on youtube occasionally, a treasure trove of memories I have captured - the laughter shared, the passions pursued and the challenges overcome.

Writing feels totally different, a skill hard to master but with each word that flows I feel a sense of liberation as I capture my memories of life's fleeting moments.

For me it's going to be a new portal to relive my cherished moments, reflect on life's lessons and express my innermost thoughts. I hope to make a deeper connection with myself and the world around me. Photograph available @ MukeshDaily on Instagram.

————————————————————

Saving A Fallen Tree
April 14, 2023 #Journal
Under the scorching desert sun, I stood beside the fallen Mulberry tree, its branches still adorned with green leaves despite its unfortunate fate. Last month due to heavy wind this tree fell down but managed to survive, thanks to a few remaining roots that had held on to the earth.

That was until my bhuaji, my father's sister, visited us yesterday. She is known for her proactive nature and her belief in taking action rather than just talking. When I shared my idea of replanting the tree with her today, she immediately lent her support and wisdom to the cause. She saw the potential in saving the fallen tree and was determined to make it happen.

With her guidance, we gathered our tools and set out to replant the tree. We dug a wide and deep hole at a new spot. Using a tractor and a sturdy rope, we carefully pulled the fallen tree towards the new spot. With great care we placed the tree in the hole making sure it stood upright. We then poured sand around the roots to anchor it firmly in place.

Even the children, who were usually busy with their play, were captivated by the sight of the fallen tree being replanted. My brother fetched buckets of water and we poured it over the roots, quenching the tree's thirst after its ordeal.

It is a reminder that sometimes, in the face of adversity, all it takes is a little initiative and action to make a difference. The fallen tree had found a new lease on life and our family had found a renewed appreciation for the beauty and resilience of nature.

Photograph available @ MukeshDaily on Instagram.

————————————————————

Writing, in all its forms, is a timeless pursuit. Poetry, literature and storytelling allow individuals to express their thoughts, emotions and experiences. The written word endures through books, poems and narratives that capture the essence of their time.

Just remember there is more to life, you don't have to do it everyday. But life will be much better if you have some form of creative hobby or interest. Not for consumption but for creation.

Arts

Just about every home has some form of art adorning its walls. So, why not yours? Why not turn your space into a canvas for your own artistic expression? You don't have to be a professional artist to make it happen. Why not start with a captivating landscape photograph, one that you take yourself? It's a manageable goal and it's entirely achievable. Let your home reflect your own creativity and style!

Painting, drawing and sculpture have been cherished creative pursuits for centuries. The beauty of visual arts lies in their ability to convey emotions, tell stories and reflect the world's beauty and complexity.

Music

Sound is powerful. Rhythm is powerful. Music is an example. You can debate an intellectual but I have hardly seen anyone debating an artist, a musician or a poet. That's powerful.

The creation and appreciation of music, whether through playing instruments, composing or simply listening, is a timeless creative pursuit that speaks to the soul. Music has the power to evoke powerful emotions and connect people across time and space.

Poetry

The writing and appreciation of poetry has persisted throughout history. Poetry is a condensed and emotionally charged form of expression, allowing words to be crafted into beautiful and evocative compositions.

Dance

Dance is a universal language of expression, blending physical movement with artistic interpretation. From traditional folk dances to contemporary choreography, it remains a beloved creative pursuit for self-expression and cultural celebration.

Theater

Theater allows actors and performers to bring stories to life on stage. Drama, comedy, and other forms of live performance continue to captivate audiences.

CHAPTER EIGHT

SPIRITUAL

Explorations & Experiences

Spiritual pursuits is an affirmation of the boundless yearning of the human spirit. It is a journey into the depths of the soul, a quest for connection with the divine and an embrace of the mysteries that lie beyond the material world. It is a rebellion against the emptiness of materialism, a revolt against the superficial and a declaration that you are not just a biological entity but a vessel of the divine.

So, why should you have a spiritual pursuit? Because life is too profound to be lived in shallowness when it can be experienced in the depths of the sacred. Because your spirit yearns for the connection only it can establish, the wisdom only it can comprehend and the transcendence only it can achieve. Because a spiritual pursuit is not a pastime; it is a lifeline to the boundless expanse of the spiritual realm, a journey of enlightenment and a celebration of the extraordinary depth of the human soul.

In the act of spiritual exploration, you become the mystic of your own existence, the sage of your own wisdom and the luminary of your own spiritual odyssey.

In a world that prioritizes external success and material wealth, the pursuit of self offers a counterbalance, it's the intimate exploration of one's essence.

The spiritual pursuit of self is a deeply personal and a lifelong journey that involves seeking a profound understanding of one's true nature, purpose and connection to the universe or a higher power.

It is the quest for self-awareness, enlightenment and inner peace. This pursuit transcends religious boundaries and is more about exploring the inner dimensions of one's being.

It's the search for self. It's about shedding the layers of conditioning and false beliefs to reveal the pure essence of the self. It is the art of letting go, where attachment to external appearances is replaced by the serenity of the inner world. It is an unveiling of the self, like a portrait gradually taking shape on the canvas, layer by layer. Balance your involvement in a community with moments of solitude. Solitude allows you to go inward and deepen your connection with your inner self.

It's the connection with the universe. Many seekers believe in a profound connection between the self and the universe. In this view, individuals see themselves as part of a greater cosmic whole. Nature offers a sense of serenity and interconnectedness with the universe. Use these moments to connect with the natural world and self.

It's the integration of mind, body & soul as one indivisible. Practices such as yoga and meditation aim to create balance and unity within the individual. It's the process to delve deep into the consciousness, to quiet the tempestuous winds of the mind and to witness our thoughts and emotions as they emerge.

Meditation is a profound and ancient practice that has transcended generations and cultures, offering a gateway to inner peace, self-awareness and spiritual growth. It is both an art and a science of stillness, a means to explore the boundless realms of the mind and spirit. The practice of meditation can be as simple as finding a quiet space, taking a comfortable posture and focusing on the breath or a chosen point of concentration.

Explorations & Experiences

The Power of Nature

Make the mountains, the forests, the deserts and the oceans the backdrop for your soul's journey. The pursuit is not about escaping reality but embracing it in all its complexity and beauty.

Nature plays a significant role in our adventurous and exploratory journeys. The natural world with its grandeur and mystery has the power to awaken the spirit and instill a profound sense of interconnectedness. It is in the heart of nature that many spiritual revelations occur.

In the solitude of the wilderness or in unfamiliar lands, one can dive deep into introspection, shedding the noise of daily life and listening to the whispers of the soul.

The Call for Adventure

You know, there's something truly special about mountains. They're referred to as a place for spiritual pursuit and it's not something you can easily put into words; it's something you have to experience for yourself. Mountains are grand, rugged and challenging to climb and when you stand atop one, gazing out at the world below, it touches your soul in a way that's hard to describe. It's like a spiritual achievement, a deeply satisfying experience.

Let me share a little story with you about me and my wife's adventure of climbing Hampta Pass with our baby.

A few years back, my wife, our 2-year-old baby and I embarked on a week-long journey to Himachal during the new year. Among our plans was a day trip to Hampta Pass. Situated at 14,000 feet in Himachal Pradesh, Hampta Pass is one of those rare, breathtaking pass crossings in the Himalayas. On one side you have the lush green valley of Kullu, with its forests, grasslands and blooming flowers lining the trail. On the other side you encounter the arid, stark landscape of Lahaul with barren mountains and very little vegetation.

We hadn't initially planned for a trek since we were traveling with family. However our journey took an unexpected turn when our cars got stuck midway due to heavy snowfall. With no other options we made the decision to climb the pass and what an incredible adventure it turned out to be. We found ourselves walking on steep, towering hills with snow on one side and dry grass on the other. The bottom of the hill was deep and the top was so high, they were invisible. I was in awe as my wife took it upon herself to carry our baby all the way to the top.

It took us a few hours to make that ascent but it was a journey we might have missed if our plans had gone smoothly. You see, the human spirit yearns for challenges, for something greater. It craves the feeling of limitlessness. Adventures and challenges are how we test ourselves and discover what we're truly capable of.

Adventure has an innate allure that beckons the curious and the courageous. It is the call of the unknown, the thrill of venturing beyond the familiar and the promise of self-discovery.

Both physical adventures and spiritual quests are fraught with challenges. Overcoming these challenges, whether external or internal, instills resilience, patience and strength. It's a reminder that the path to spiritual growth is not always smooth but it is always transformative.

Adventure and exploration require a willingness to embrace the unknown. In the same way, spiritual seekers must relinquish the safety of the known and venture into the uncharted territory of their inner world. It is a courageous act of self-confrontation and transformation.

During exploration we encounters with different cultures, belief systems and worldviews. These experiences broaden our perspective and provide insights into the diversity of human experiences and the interconnectedness of all beings.

Embrace The Ancient

During our Himachal trip we stumbled upon this remarkable place, Gurudwara Manikaran Sahib, just 4 kilometers from Kasol, a leisurely walk along the Parvati River.

Now, what makes this Gurudwara truly extraordinary is the natural wonder it holds. Even in sub-zero temperatures, there's a hot water spring. These thermal waters emerge from the granite formations in this part of the Himalayan foothills. Not only are they rich in medicinal properties but the surroundings are simply breathtaking, making each hot spring in Himachal a unique experience.

But here's where it gets even more special – this famous Gurudwara is home to these hot water springs. And what's truly amazing is that they use this naturally heated water to cook the langar, the community meal served to visitors. The langar is available round the clock, offering not just nourishment but a sense of community.

And that's not all - they provide free food, free access to hot water swimming pools and free accommodation for those who visit. It's all about selfless service.

What's more remarkable is the Hot Cave within the Gurudwara premises. It's a place where people can sit and experience natural healing, potentially alleviating a variety of ailments.

This is where the spiritual aspect truly shines through. The selfless service and generosity of this community, providing not just for the soul but for the well-being of the body, is what makes Gurudwara Manikaran Sahib a truly remarkable and spiritually enriching place.

I'm sure you have had the opportunity to explore many ancient temples, churches, mosques, synagogues, monasteries and other sacred places. Have you ever stopped to think about what it feels like to be in such places? Take a moment to reflect on that. Take a look at those ancient sacred places. They exude an undeniable serenity and an ambiance that's nothing short of magical. When you step inside you can sense that the atmosphere is different and it's undeniably powerful. Most of these sites are strategically built atop hills and reaching them is no easy feat. It's almost as if they demand something from those who seek to visit them.

There's an inherent mystique and allure about these age-old structures. They've weathered the ages, standing as silent witnesses to the passage of time. The craftsmanship and devotion that our ancestors poured into their construction is truly awe inspiring. Each of these sacred places have unique stories to tell. They are shrouded in history and mystery, carrying the whispers of the past within their walls. We can't just ignore that.

You walk the path illuminated by the teachings of sages who have bequeathed their insights, their devotion and their transcendent wisdom to light your way. Whether it's visiting ancient temples, meditating on mountaintops or exploring sacred sites, these journeys often lead to a deeper understanding of one's place in the cosmos.

In the realm of spirituality, you become a pilgrim, a seeker and a disciple of the cosmos.

CHAPTER NINE

LEADERSHIP

"A man without a vision shall perish."

Life is like building a pyramid. It's a gradual process that unfolds over time. Just think about it – each layer of the pyramid represents a dimension of your life and you build them one by one, patiently and persistently.

No one is going to hand you a manual for living; you're the architect of your own life. And if you look at it in a positive light, I'd like to share my story to illustrate. I'm far from perfect, just like a pyramid being built, I'm a work in progress.

No one sat me down and said, "Hey, focus on your health and fitness". Nope, that was a journey I embarked on my own. Nobody told me to do cycling, set up a gym or strive for an athletic body.

Intellectual expression? When it comes to intellectual growth, there was no one there to give me a checklist. Journaling, building a home library and writing a book were all pursuits I carved out for myself.

Artistic expression? Nobody held my hand through it. I decided to pick up a camera, venture into photography & filmmaking and start my own YouTube channel.

Spiritual expression? Now, the topic of spiritual growth might raise a few eyebrows but it's a personal journey that no one can define for you. Some may see it as a joke but it's all about your unique understanding of life. We can only truly relate to and realize in others what's already within us. We can never truly see what we're not.

When it comes to family, legacy, generational wealth, family businesses and brotherhood those are the paths that I discovered independently and are work in progress. In fact brainwashed people are against the ideas of family. I'll talk about that in great length in the next section.

Sure, along the way, you'll hear inspiring ideas and you'll make great associations. But remember, in the end, it's up to you to lead your own life. Embrace the journey, build your own pyramid and make it a masterpiece that reflects your unique vision and aspirations.

No matter what you do and who you are, you must be the leader of your life. Lead every aspect of your life, including professional. You might be an employee but you must lead and create your own path. Leadership is not optional. A man without vision shall perish essentially means a man who isn't leading his life will perish. It's all about taking charge of your life, setting the course and being the captain of your own ship.

So, what does leading your own life mean? Well, it's about being your own CEO, the boss of your own life. It starts with self awareness - understanding who you are, your values, strengths, weaknesses and what makes you tick. Know yourself inside and out. Understand yourself. Once you've got that self-awareness down, it's about setting clear goals. It's like charting a course for your journey, so you know where you're headed. Discipline is the backbone of self leadership. Discipline keeps you on course, helping you make the right choices, stick to your goals and resist distractions and temptations. You've got to take care of yourself physically and mentally. It's about getting enough rest, eating well, exercising and managing stress. A well-maintained ship sails farther and better. Time management helps you make the most of your journey, ensuring you're using your time wisely and prioritizing what matters most.

Life's an unpredictable sea and you'll encounter storms and calm waters. Being adaptable means adjusting your sails when the winds change and being open to new opportunities and ways of doing things. Resilience is about bouncing back from setbacks and staying afloat, no matter how tough the waters get. Every setback is a lesson in disguise. Self reflection is your compass. Regularly check in with yourself. Are you still heading in the right direction? What have you learned along the way? It's all part of the journey. And don't forget to celebrate your victories. Even the small ones. It's like marking the islands you've discovered along your journey. Acknowledge how far you've come. It boosts positive energy.

Once you can lead your life and your family, you can lead teams, communities and even nations. This time there are more people on the ship. Leaders are like the captain of the ship, guiding it through uncharted waters. It's about more than just being the boss or giving orders. It's about inspiring, guiding and empowering others to reach their full potential and achieve a common goal. No matter what the purpose is, if you have got people together, someone will lead. If you have some bigger purpose, you will need people to achieve that and you have to lead. No group can survive and thrive without leadership. It's not a question of why but who?

No matter how good you are at something, if you don't have good communication skills, you will never achieve your full potential in the world. Communication is the lifeblood of our interactions with others. Communication has evolved with civilization and it acts like a bridge that connects us to others, allowing us to share ideas, thoughts and emotions. Not just words but sounds, rhythms, vibes and your own body language. Your body speaks volumes. The way you maintain eye contact, use gestures and stand or sit all plays a role in communication. The moment you open your mouth, you tell the world who you are. People judge by how you speak and leadership is about people. It's not a question of right or wrong, it's the reality. It's through leadership that you can shape lives and destinies.

Have A Vision

I think of vision holistically. Vision for self, vision for my family and a vision for my role in the world. This book is written out of a vision of my life, as you read, it will become quite evident.

Dream big, take the time to craft your vision and communicate it with passion. It's true that there is no passion to be found playing small. People are miserable when they don't feel like they are working on something meaningful, something big. It's our tendency to be unlimited, to be big, to do big and to achieve big.

Leaders have a clear vision and the ability to articulate it. They can inspire others by sharing their vision of the future with compelling storytelling and explaining how their efforts contribute to that vision. Having a vision requires strategic thinking. Think of strategic thinking as zooming out from the map. It's about seeing the forest, not just the trees.

Your vision is the north on your leadership compass, leading you to uncharted territories and exciting adventures. Creating a vision involves thinking about the long-term impact of your leadership. It's about making a difference that lasts, not just short-term gains. But remember, a vision is not set in stone. It's a living, breathing entity. It can evolve as you grow and as circumstances change. Be flexible but stay true to your core values and purpose.

Look around, the majority don't have any vision for anything. They need a vision, a leader to lead them. If not you, someone will lead and someone is already leading. Have a vision if you want to lead.

Build Your Team

Back in 2019, I found myself knee-deep in the world of esports, organizing esports tournaments daily. It was a wild ride, let me tell you. I had this massive Discord community with a whopping 10,000 players. We had over 1000 squads, not to mention duos and solos all raring to compete. On any given day, we had around 100 teams duking it out in our tournaments.

Now, here's the kicker. I was just one person and trying to manage all those teams, the casting, the streaming. But the beauty of it all was that our community was built on pure passion for gaming and esports. So, many amazing folks stepped up and volunteered their time and skills. It was a beautiful thing; we kept this esport tournaments going strong for nearly a whole year. Of course, we did need some extra hands where the going got tough and that's when we decided to bring in some paid help. But the rest of the magic, the heart and soul of it, that was all volunteer work.

That, My friend, is the power of volunteer work. It's how many social endeavors roll. We've got folks pitching in, not because they have to but because they want to. It's a stark contrast to the corporate world where it's all about paychecks and contracts.

In the end, no matter what you're up to, it's your people, your team, all united in a common mission and that's the real secret sauce to making things happen.

Building a team of the right people is one of the most important skills of a leader. Leaders pick the right people, foster collaboration and create a strong sense of unity. It's like they're building a well-oiled machine that runs on trust and respect. Carefully select team members to build a cohesive and high-performing team on a shared purpose.

Consider what roles are needed to achieve your goals. What specific skills and expertise are required? It's like assembling a diverse group of characters for your story. Look for people who possess the skills, experience and passion that align with your vision. Think of it as choosing individuals who are eager to go on this adventure along with you and your team.

A great leader is a master communicator. They know how to listen, share ideas and motivate their team. They're not just talking heads; they're storytellers, sharing a vision of the future and showing how everyone's efforts fit into that grand vision. Paint a compelling picture of the future and explain how everyone's efforts contribute to that vision. No great team can be built without communicating the vision.

The ability to persuade and influence others is a critical leadership skill. Leaders can motivate and inspire by their words and actions. Influence is their superpower. Even without a fancy title, they can persuade and motivate others. They inspire through words and actions making the impossible seem attainable. Inspire and motivate others, even without formal authority. Lead through your words and actions. People are naturally attracted to influencers. That can make it easy to find people who would like to join you.

A leader trusts their team to handle tasks and responsibilities. It's about empowerment and focusing on the bigger picture. Build a team you can trust and delegate to them what you can. You have to trust your team to handle responsibilities and tasks. Delegation empowers your team and frees you up for higher-level priorities.

Lead Your Team

"More is lost by indecision than wrong decision. Indecision is the thief of opportunity. It will steal

you blind." - Marcus Tullius Cicero

Strategic thinking is their roadmap to success. As a leader you must consider the long game, making plans and aligning actions with your team's goals. It's all about the bigger picture. Develop long-term plans and align your actions with your bigger goal. Consider the big picture and lead with purpose. Consider your moves in the context of your competitors and seek ways to gain an advantage. Like a detective, gather and analyze information to make informed decisions. Identify potential risks and challenges and develop contingency plans to navigate them. Naturally everyone has some level of this skill but think about a general or a CEO, your natural skills will fall short against theirs. If you are playing big games, you will need professional level skills.

Decisions, decisions! Leaders are the decision-makers, the ones who take the plunge when things get tough. They don't shy away from problems; they tackle them head-on and find creative solutions. They're like problem-solving wizards. If you can't make decisions with speed and strategy, you can't lead effectively. Modern world competes on the motto of "Move fast and break things". If a decision doesn't have the possibility of a significant negative impact and can be reversed, make it and move fast.

A leader has to be adaptable. There is no fixed formula. You will prove wrong time and time again. Change is the only constant and leaders are the ones who navigate those unpredictable waters. They're flexible, open to new ideas and ready to pivot when needed. Change is inevitable and leaders who can navigate through uncertainty are more successful. Be adaptable and open to new ideas.

Time management is their secret to productivity. It's hard to manage one's time. Now think about when a group of people are involved. Personal time management must be a personal responsibility. Leaders are like time wizards, managing their schedules, prioritizing tasks and focusing on what really matters. Prioritize tasks and focus on what's most important. Effective time management sets the pace for your team. When everyone is clear about the priorities, everyone will use their time accordingly.

Leaders take responsibility for their decisions and actions and they also hold their team members accountable for their commitments. Ownership means responsibility and responsibility demands accountability. Provide constructive guidance which can help your team members reach their full potential and achieve your common goal. It's like nurturing a garden.

The best way to lead is to lead by example. Your actions speak louder than words. Set a positive example by demonstrating the values and behaviors you expect from your team. Your focus, commitment and energy is what will inspire others to do the same.

Empathy helps leaders understand their people, because it's all about people. They understand their own emotions and those of their team members. Leaders can step into someone else's shoes and see the world from their perspective. This empathy helps them connect with people on a deeper level and build strong, lasting relationships. Don't just talk; listen. Actively listening to your team members helps build trust and allows you to better understand their needs and concerns. Understand the emotions and perspectives of your team members. Show empathy and build strong, genuine relationships.

Motivation is the fuel that drives a leader's team. They know how to inspire, using recognition, rewards or simply setting a positive example. They keep the fire burning under everyone's feet. Use various strategies to motivate your team, whether through recognition, rewards or simply offering praise and encouragement. Inspire your team with a sense of purpose. Be clear, concise and open in your communication and always encourage feedback.

Conflicts are bound to happen where there are people. But leaders know how to handle them, the ones who bring harmony back when the going gets tough. They mediate disputes and find solutions that keep the team on the same page. Address conflicts constructively and aim for win-win solutions. A harmonious team is a productive one.

In times of crisis, leaders are calm in the storm. They handle the chaos, make tough decisions and lead their team through adversity. Be prepared to manage crises and make decisions under pressure. Maintain your composure and guide your team through adversity. Resilience is like their suit of armor. Bounce back from setbacks, learn from failures and keep moving forward, no matter what. Your ability to persevere sets the tone for your team.

Cultivate A Network

Over the years, I've had the chance to connect with hundreds of industry leaders in technology space. It's been quite a journey. However, the thing is, there was often no common ground for us to collaborate on anything. So, all those connections remained somewhat dormant.

This year I started my journey as a consultant in the technology space. I began to share my industry knowledge and technical expertise with others and I extended a helping hand wherever I could. Now, I am recognized as one of the top voices in the industry. Many industry leaders have started following and reaching out to me, seeking my advice and insights.

For me networking wasn't relevant until it suddenly became. I feel that I should have started this journey way earlier. Building connections, trust and credibility as an independent consultant takes time. But I know that it's going to take a lot more time and effort before I can truly see any return.

Think of networking as relationship-building. It's not about what others can do for you but how you can create mutually beneficial connections. Nurture these relationships like you would a valued friendship. Networking opens doors of opportunities. A strong network sometimes will act as a support network.

Think strategically about your networking efforts. What are your goals and how can your network help you achieve them? You are plotting a course for your journey. You will be building a wide network to gather valuable connections, insights and opportunities. Networking isn't just about collecting business cards; it's about expanding your horizons. Connect with people from diverse backgrounds, industries and experiences.

The most valuable insights often come from listening. Ask questions, be genuinely interested and learn from others. You are literally gathering wisdom from the stories of fellow travelers. Be well informed about industry trends and changes. Just as a wise traveler researches the path ahead, staying informed helps you make informed decisions. Share your expertise, provide referrals and introductions and share your knowledge. It's a two way street.

Each leader is unique. Leaders take initiatives, nobody tells a leader to lead. Leadership is not just a title; it's a set of skills and qualities that make a difference in people's lives. It's the art of guiding and inspiring others to reach new heights and conquer the challenges that come their way. Be open to learning and evolving your leadership style to suit the needs of your team and the challenges you face.

Call to Action - Self

Holistic and Honorable

Cultivate Strength of Character.

Train like a Warrior.

Think Like a Sage.

Create like an Artist.

Be like a Monk.

Lead Your Life, Your Family and Your People.

II. Family: Provide & Protect

Remember Self is Temporal but Family is Generational.

Now shift the focus to Family. It's like a warm hug from the universe emphasizing the importance of providing and protecting. Brotherhood, here, is like a cozy blanket on a chilly day, reminding you that you're not alone in this grand adventure.

CHAPTER TEN

FAMILY

"Before there was any society, religion, market or nation, there was family."

Most people don't value what they have. Most people don't realize the value of family until it's too late. We're constantly running after these big dreams and aspirations and in the process we kind of forget to savor those little moments of happiness that we ought to be sharing with our loved ones. Time has a way of slipping through our fingers and those moments, those people, they won't be around forever.

Think about death holistically. My sincere wish for you and your loved ones is a long and fulfilling life. Now let's delve into some theoretical discussion.

When we ponder the idea of death, we focus on our own mortality. You've probably heard the question posed from various sources: "What if today were your last day?" It's a thought provoking question, no doubt. However, I invite you to consider another more important scenario: "What if today were the last day for someone in your family?" This scenario becomes particularly more important if you're not the eldest member of your family. We all have families and the truth is - our family members won't be with us forever.

Naturally, as time passes, our parents, in particular, move closer to the end of their lives. Yet, we tend to overlook this fact and primarily focus on our own mortality. What about our parents and other family members? They have played pivotal roles in shaping our lives and have had a profound impact on us. This perspective helps us realign our priorities. Cherish and appreciate the people who have been there for you and to make the most of the time you have with them.

Honor Your Ancestors. Embrace the sacred duty of honoring your Ancestors, they are the first and foremost, the foundation of your existence was laid upon their sweat, blood and sacrifices. Remember them.

Honor Your Parents. To honor your parents is to acknowledge the architects of your earliest memories and the guardians of your tender dreams. Within their embrace, we find not only the shelter but also the rich story of their love and sacrifices.

The pages of life's story are turned with the wisdom of age. Showing reverence to those who have tread upon more chapters is not only a sign of respect but a tribute to the wisdom they bestow, It's honorable.

As we travel through our lives, remember that blood ties run deeper than any river and the bonds of childhood form the bedrock of our character.

Honor Your Brothers & Sisters. Let us not forget the dear souls who shared our childhood dreams and secrets. They are the keepers of our secrets and the companions of our youth. In their presence, we find the warm hearth of shared memories and the shelter of unfaltering support. Acknowledge their presence in your life, treasure the irreplaceable moments and nurture the connection that transcends time and distance.

With each sunrise and sunset, find within yourself the love and honor for your spouse. Our connection with our spouse is more than a vacation; it's a lifelong journey. We don't treat our spouse as a mere visitor, someone to turn to only in times of need or distress. Instead, we coexist and thrive together, sharing our lives in a meaningful way. We need to engage in conversations that go beyond the surface and explore the depths of our thoughts and feelings.

Family is where you come from. It's your roots, your foundation. It's where you learn your very first lessons in life – how to walk, how to talk, how to be a decent human being. It's your parents or guardians who guide you through those early years, helping you navigate the rocky waters of childhood.

It's where you find comfort and support. When the world outside gets a little too tough to handle, you know you can always turn to your family. They're the ones who'll catch you when you fall and lift you up when you're down.

It's in the small moments, too – like those family dinners where everyone gathers around the table to share stories and laughter. Or those movie nights when you're all huddled up on the couch, arguing about what to watch. Even the disagreements and arguments, which, let's be honest, are bound to happen, are a part of the family experience. It's all a part of the messy, beautiful family life.

It's a source of love, laughter and a whole lot of life lessons. It's a place where you can be yourself, flaws and all and still find acceptance.

You know, it's kinda heartbreaking how often people miss out on the real essence of family life. We get so caught up in the never-ending pursuit of success, the rat race and the grand achievements that we tend to overlook the simple, little secrets of life.

We're running tirelessly, chasing those big pleasures and material gains, sometimes to the point where family takes a back seat. Success becomes the sole definition of our lives. We want to be the brightest student in the class, climb that corporate ladder, be the most ambitious soul out there.

But in this pursuit, we often forget what truly matters. We neglect our families, the very people who have been with us through thick and thin. It's like family becomes an afterthought, not even a priority.

Some even dive into marriages without the love and emotional connection that should be at its core. They end up leading separate lives under the same roof, distant and disconnected. It's like they're so entangled in their individual pursuits that they forget what brought them together in the first place.

Life's about balance, you know? It's about realizing that success is not just about professional achievements. It's also about the warmth of your family, the love you share and the moments you create together. There is no success if we miss out on the little secrets of life while we chase the big pleasures. Make family a priority, a place of love and connection, rather than a footnote in the story of our lives.

You know, one of the harsh realities of life is that family isn't forever. It changes, it evolves and as time marches on, it also grows old and well, eventually, we all must face the inevitable – death.

Your family, the people you hold dear, they won't be the same forever. Those kids you have, the ones who are running around causing chaos, they won't be kids for long. They'll grow, they'll change and you'll look back and wonder where all that time went.

Your parents, those who've cared for you, nurtured you, they won't be here with us forever. It's a tough reality to accept but it's the truth. And even your spouse, the person you chose to share your life with, they won't remain the same either. Time has a way of molding and shaping us all.

Time, well, it's a bit like death in its own way. It's a constant, a ticking clock that doesn't stop for anyone. It's taking away bits of our lives with every passing second. It's not until we reach the end of the road that we often truly realize the importance of family.

We spend our younger years, often carefree and sometimes wasting time on things that don't really matter. We take our family for granted, thinking they'll always be there. But in the end, we might find ourselves wishing we had made more of those moments count, that we had valued our family more.

In the end, sometimes, we have no choice. Time moves forward and we must move with it. So, it's worth remembering, in the grand scheme of things, family is one of life's most precious gifts and it's important to cherish it while we have the chance.

Being constantly busy can really take a toll on your family. It's like, if you have a precious 30 minutes of free time, what do you do with it? Do you let it be, savor the freedom? No, most of us tend to fill it with yet more tasks and distractions.

But it's in those rare moments of tranquility, those pockets of free time, that you start to grasp what's truly important. Your priorities get a quick reshuffling and you realize, "Hey, maybe I should just sit back and enjoy this short break."

We often find ourselves spending more time scrolling through social media than being with our own family. We get so caught up in the virtual world that we forget the real one right in front of us.

But you see, when life starts flashing before your eyes and you're in the final moments, what do you remember most? It's your family. Nothing else really matters at that point. It's your loved ones who are there with you, by your side and it's your family who'll continue to feel the pain long after you're gone.

All those big dreams and ambitions you were relentlessly chasing? Well, they sort of take a back seat when it comes down to it. They become secondary. What matters most, what should matter most, is your family. So, why not make them a priority right now? Because right now, you still have a choice. In the end, you won't. Your family, they should always be front and center.

Alright, let's talk about making time for family. It's not always easy, especially in our fast-paced, busy lives. But here's the deal, it's super important. Your family deserves your time and attention. So, let's dive into some practical ways to make that happen:

First things first, you've got to make it a priority. Just like you'd prioritize a work meeting or a deadline. Block out specific time slots for family activities and stick to them. One of the mistakes ambitious people make is, they fill their life with work and then more work. Don't overcommit yourself. You need free time, free time for self and free time for family. Sometimes, you've got to say no to other commitments. It's okay to decline invitations or reschedule non-urgent tasks to make space for family.

Use your time wisely. Get organized, set goals and manage your time effectively. This can help you become more efficient, freeing up time for your family. You don't have to do everything yourself. Split work if needed, Share if it can work. It lightens your load and allows more time for bonding.

Look around your family, we're constantly glued to screens. Make it a rule to unplug during family time. Put away your phones, turn off the TV and be fully present. Quality time matters more than screen time. Family dinners are a fantastic tradition. Try to have dinner together. It's the best way to get together to catch up, share stories and connect with your loved ones. Some intellectuals wonder why we celebrate! They don't know what a family is. Don't forget to celebrate birthdays, anniversaries and other special occasions. These are opportunities to create cherished memories with your family. Plan fun outings or activities as a family. Whether it's a weekend trip, a visit to a park or a simple game night at home, these experiences create lasting memories.

It's not about being perfect; it's about showing that you care. When you're with your family, be truly present. Put away distractions, listen actively and engage in meaningful conversations. Quality time is all about the quality of your presence. So, go ahead and start carving out that time for the people who matter most in your life.

It's in these little everyday, ordinary moments that we find the extraordinary love, connection and happiness that family brings. Cherish these moments, for they are the true treasures of family life.

There's something beautiful about starting your day with a hug and a kiss from your loved ones. It sets the tone for a positive day ahead. Those unexpected hugs from your children or a loving embrace from your spouse can brighten even the toughest days. Small acts of kindness within the family, like making a surprise breakfast or leaving a sweet note, are like little love tokens.

Nothing beats a homemade meal enjoyed as a family. It's not just about the food; it's about the conversations, the bonding and the love that goes into it. Whether it's a silly joke, a funny story or just a spontaneous burst of laughter at the dinner table, those shared moments of mirth are like a breath of fresh air. Cozying up on the couch with your family, popcorn in hand, for a movie night is a simple pleasure that's hard to beat. It's about enjoying a great film and each other's company.

Sometimes, it's the quiet moments, like sitting together in comfortable silence, that are filled with love and understanding. Reading bedtime stories to your kids or being read to by your parents is a great tradition that's filled with warmth and fond memories. When family members pitch in to help with chores, homework or simply lending a hand when someone's feeling overwhelmed, it's a beautiful display of support.

The seasons would come and go but the love within a family would remain eternal. Time can never steal a life lived full of love, joy and memories. Family and love are the most precious gifts of all. Carry it forward.

Marriage is like a canvas and the couple is the artist. Together, they create a unique masterpiece of love, devotion and companionship. Isn't it? Well, it's a different matter what they paint on it.

What makes life worth living are the moments of laughter and tears, the shared dreams and aspirations and the love that binds two souls together. Life's joys are sweeter when shared and its burdens are lighter when carried by two.

Some intellectuals will call marriage a legal contract, many will be fooled. But they forget they are not the product of a legal contract. It is love that truly makes the world go round.

No marriage is without its ups and downs. Disagreements, compromises and growing pains are all part of togetherness. It's in these moments that the strength of a relationship is tested. It's in the tough times that a strong marriage shines.

From the comfort of waking up next to each other to building a life together, that's family.

When you think about starting a family, you're taking the responsibility of a fresh new life, one that will be molded by your love, care and values. It's a decision that will change your lives in ways you can't imagine.

It isn't just about choosing to bring a new life into the world. It will redefine your priorities. It will test your limits. It's also about embracing a life full of sleepless nights, diaper changes and a whirlwind of emotions.

Children have the power to fill your life with boundless love, laughter and a sense of purpose. They bring with them the promise of new beginnings and the opportunity to witness the world through fresh, innocent eyes.

You cradle a fragile, squirming bundle of life and suddenly your world shifts. From that moment on your heart will walk around outside your body. You'll witness the miracle of first steps, the magic of first words, the power of a child's laughter and the cuteness of a child.

Parenthood isn't just about ensuring your child's survival; it's about nurturing their dreams, quirks and personality. It's about growing together. As they learn about the world, you rediscover it through their eyes. It's a paradoxical blend of frustration and fulfillment, self-doubt and self-discovery.

Parenthood is a book with no final chapter, parents will be parents forever. Their child will be their child forever.

The connection between a mother and her child is profound and unbreakable. It's a bond that transcends time and distance. Her love is the foundation upon which children build their futures. In a world filled with uncertainty, a mother's embrace is a sanctuary of warmth and assurance.

Motherhood is the act of selflessness, unconditional love and sacrifices. It's the ability to put a child's needs above one's own to nourish not just with sustenance but with wisdom, care and unconditional affection.

Mothers are the guardians of the earliest memories, the healers of scraped knees and the comforters in the darkest of nights.

A father is not just a provider but a mentor and a source of strength. In a world full of challenges, fathers provide stability and security for their children.

Fathers offer a different perspective, complementing the nurturing nature of mothers. They bring balance to parenting, offering their children a broader view of the world. Through their actions and interactions, fathers demonstrate respect, integrity and the importance of hard work.

Nothing is more painful for a child than to be raised without a father or a mother. It's a pain of a lifetime. And that requires a guardian of extraordinary love, care and values.

Deep down everyone loves their family and children. You want nothing but the absolute best for them. You yearn to be there as your kids grow up and as your parents grow older. Yet you also crave some time for yourself - to travel, exercise, meet friends, watch great movies and dive into your hobbies.

The thing is, a significant chunk of your waking hours is either spent working or thinking about how to excel in your job. Sometimes, it's in a high-pressure, intense environment. But you refuse to let your job define you or reduce your life to a mere task list.

So here's the real question: what takes precedence - your career or your family? It's a no-brainer, isn't it? Family should always come first. However, it's surprising how many people fall into the trap of putting work before family. Yes, work is important but it's the order of priorities that truly matters because it shapes the course of your life. Trust me, it's a colossal regret to work your entire life without ever putting family first. Your kids won't be kids forever. Your parents won't be here forever. You can't catch them where you left them.

Make a commitment to your family both at home and in your workplace. Here's a golden piece of advice that holds true in all aspects of life: if you don't protect what's yours, others will take it away. That's how the world works, that's the harsh reality. You've got to safeguard what you hold dear – your time, your family, your resources and everything.

Take deliberate actions when it comes to achieving a work-life balance and stick to your decisions. Set clear boundaries with people and establish goals not just for your work but also for your family. Remember you're the only one who can truly protect what you care about because everyone else is busy safeguarding their own interests.

Now here's a gem of wisdom: the greatest gift parents can give to their children is their time. Find creative ways to be present both physically and emotionally for your children. Your love and attention will be the pillars upon which they build their futures. So, in the grand juggling act of life, let family remain at the forefront. Your heart will thank you for it.

When it comes to spending quality time with your kids, it's all about creating meaningful moments that strengthen your bond and make lasting memories.

First and foremost, put away those distractions. Turn off the TV, put down your phone and disconnect from the outside world. Give your children your full attention. It might sound easy but in our fast-paced lives it can be a challenge.

Get down to their level. Whether you're playing with action figures, drawing pictures or building a house with blankets, get on the floor and engage with them on their turf. This shows them that their world matters to you.

Share stories. Whether it's reading a book together or making up your own stories, the power of storytelling is magical. It ignites their imagination and creates a special connection between you and your child.

Explore the great outdoors. Take a walk in the park, go for a bike ride or have a picnic. Nature has a wonderful way of stimulating curiosity and sparking conversations.

Cook together. Whip up a batch of cookies or try a new recipe. In the kitchen, you can teach them valuable life skills and the end result is a delicious treat you both can enjoy.

Encourage their interests. Whether they love painting, playing music or even a particular sport, show genuine interest in what they're passionate about. Attend their games or recitals and cheer them on.

Plan special one-on-one time. It's important to spend time with each child individually. This makes them feel valued and important, strengthening your relationship with them.

Listen actively. When your child wants to talk, be an attentive listener. Ask open-ended questions and let them express themselves. This not only builds trust but also provides opportunities for guidance and support.

Teach them life skills. Involve your kids in everyday tasks like gardening, laundry or fixing things around the house. These activities not only teach them valuable skills but also provide quality time together.

Kids grow up so fast and these moments are precious. Cherish them, laugh with them and create a loving environment where they can thrive. Be present in the moment.

Home

Imagine a home adorned with a garden of tropical plants, a small pond filled with colorful fishes and a gentle stream of water trickling by. Doesn't that sound like a dream home, in its own unique way?

And the best part is, it's not one of those luxury homes. Nope, it's a natural haven, brimming with life, not with material possessions. Your home becomes a thriving garden of life, a place where your family flourishes and truly lives. It's not about things; it's about embracing the beauty of nature right at your doorstep.

I have spent quite a good amount of time helping my wife collect some amazing plants. We love plants. They're a little piece of nature that makes a house feel like a home.

Home plants are like a breath of fresh air in our daily lives. They come in all shapes and sizes and they each have their own personality. You can place them on windowsills, hang them from

Home is where you dream, where you plan and where you grow together as a family. It's not just a place; it's an embodiment of love, safety and togetherness. Home is where you can be your true self, where you're accepted and loved unconditionally. It's the smell of a home-cooked meal, the sound of laughter echoing through the halls and the warmth of a cozy blanket on a rainy day.

You see, it's not about the physical structure; it's about the people within it. It's where children take their first steps, where love is celebrated and where tears are comforted. It's where traditions are born and where secrets are shared. Now that's a special place. Home should always be a place family members don't wanna run away from.

Add your personal touch to your home. Display family photos, decorate with your favorite colors and surround yourself with things that make you happy. It's all about creating a space that reflects you and your family. Houseplants not only look great but also improve the air quality and bring a touch of nature into your home. Incorporate music and art into your home. Play your favorite tunes, display artwork that inspires you and create an environment that stimulates your senses.

Responsibility

Provide, Protect & Preserve.

There is a famous dialogue from the movie "The Magnificent Seven" that tells a lot about responsibility.

Village Boy: We're ashamed to live here. Our fathers are cowards.

O'Reilly: Don't you ever say that again about your fathers, because they are not cowards! You think I am brave because I carry a gun? Well, your fathers are much braver because they carry responsibility, for you, your brothers, your sisters and your mothers. And this responsibility is like a big rock that weighs a ton. It bends and it twists them until finally it buries them under the ground. And nobody says they have to do this. They do it because they love you and because they want to. I have never had this kind of courage. Running a farm, working like a mule every day with no guarantee anything will ever come of it. This is bravery. That's why I never even started anything like that... that's why I never will.

Here are some of the most fundamental responsibilities. World will fool you talking about happiness, fun and what not, they are the outcome, not the responsibilities in itself.

Unconditional Love

The family is a the only place for unconditional love. It's a place where, no matter the mistakes made, the door is always open, forgiveness is extended and love remains unwavering. Love is the bedrock upon which a family is built. It's the soft embrace that soothes the wounded heart, the encouraging words that lift the spirit and the unwavering support that propels each member to reach for the stars.

Financial Responsibility

While love and emotional support are vital, families also share the financial responsibilities. It's working together to provide for the household's needs and planning for the future.

Teaching and Guiding

Families are the first schools of life. Parents, siblings and grandparents are the teachers, imparting values, ethics and life lessons. They guide the younger generation toward becoming responsible and compassionate individuals.

World will fool you, manipulate you, exploit you. Only a father or a mother can guide their children. Even teachers aren't gurus. Their minds are tied to the system to teach them enough to work for society. Think about this, only your family has your best interest in their mind and heart.

Safety & Security

Families provide a shield against the harshness of the world. Like a guardian angel, they nurture their own, offering physical safety, emotional comfort and a haven where vulnerabilities are embraced rather than exploited.

It's a common sense advice but many people become so much fooled by world that they forget who is on their side and who is just using them.

Legacy

Families carry the legacy of their ancestors and create new traditions for the future. It's passing down wisdom, stories and values ensuring that the family's history and culture are preserved. Families mark the milestones and joys of life together. From birthdays to achievements, they celebrate with laughter and shared experiences, creating memories that will be cherished for generations.

CHAPTER ELEVEN

LEGACY

"Leaving a lasting legacy for your family is not about what you leave behind but the values and wisdom you pass along."

By thinking beyond our own horizons and considering the legacy we're leaving behind, we can make a profound difference in the world and ensure that our family's impact endures for generations to come.

It's about our children, our grandchildren and all those who will come after us. It's about leaving behind a world that's better than the one we inherited. It's about sowing the seeds of positive change that will continue to bear fruit long after we're gone. It's about building a legacy that inspires, empowers and uplifts those who come after us.

Families play a pivotal role in shaping the future. The values, traditions and wisdom we pass down to our descendants are like building blocks for the generations to come. We're not just living for the present; we're laying the groundwork for a brighter future.

We've got to be mindful of the planet we're leaving for our descendants. The choices we make today, in terms of sustainability and environmental stewardship, have a direct impact on the world they'll inherit. Why not plant a few trees? It takes decades for some trees to grow fully. If you plant today, your kids will have the shade one day and these trees will stay long after you are gone.

Imagine a grand, sun-drenched library, a sanctuary of knowledge and tradition, where the walls are adorned with portraits of ancestors who have contributed to the family's remarkable heritage. This library is not just a room; it's a vessel of wisdom, a keeper of stories.

The beauty of legacy is that it strengthens the bonds between generations and creates a sense of belonging and purpose that will be cherished by all. Legacy isn't static; it evolves with each generation.

Family Values & Goals

Begin by identifying the core values that your family holds dear. These values will be the foundation of your legacy. Gather your family members and have a meaningful conversation about the values you collectively cherish. Make a list of these values. Encourage everyone to express their thoughts and ensure that all voices are heard.

Establish clear family goals that align with your values. These goals could include community service, philanthropy or personal achievements. Create a vision board or a family goals journal to track progress. Assign specific responsibilities to family members based on their interests and talents.

Generational Wealth

Let's talk about generational wealth. It's not just about making money for yourself; it's about creating a legacy that benefits your family for generations to come. See, when you think about generational wealth, you're thinking long-term. It's about making wise financial decisions, investing and passing down assets and knowledge to your children and grandchildren and so on. It's like planting a money tree that'll keep bearing fruit for your family's future.

The beauty of generational wealth is that it can break the cycle of financial hardship, providing opportunities, education and a better life for your descendants. It's like building a bridge to a brighter future, ensuring that your family's financial well-being isn't just for today but for all the tomorrows to come. A successful business, family assets or a strong diverse portfolio of investments can be a significant source of generational wealth. A family business can also be a great asset for generations to come.

Family Business

Don't be fooled by the modern world on what a business is and how it should be run. World will always be anti-family. Family is the only legitimate organization. Everything else is made up, agreed upon contracts which can be broken in a fraction of a second without a second thought. I have enormous respect for family businesses.

Family businesses are built on a foundation of trust and shared values. When you work with your loved ones, there's an inherent sense of trust that can be hard to replicate in other settings.

The legacy of a family business is a profound one. It's not just about the financial bottom line; it's about passing down a piece of your family's identity to future generations. The business becomes a vessel for your family's story and that's a legacy that can be cherished and continued.

One of the beautiful aspects of family businesses is their resilience. They weather storms and adapt to change because they're not just motivated by profits but by a desire to see the family legacy continue. Families have the soul and that soul is the differentiator between corporations and family business. This can create a strong, enduring business that stays for generations. And if you have seen multi generational businesses, even if it is a small restaurant, you know the feeling.

People have a thousand reasons on why you should not start a family business. But like everything, there is a solution for most of the trivial questions. Nobody will ever tell you to start a family business, everyone will tell you to never. It will require extra efforts to manage the family image which the media and people will try to destroy for pity reasons. Keep their opinions outside the door.

Family Stories & Library

One of the most powerful ways to leave a legacy is through storytelling. Collect and document family stories, anecdotes and experiences from different generations. Encourage elders to share their life stories, lessons learned and memorable moments. Create a family history book, a digital archive or even a storytelling session during family gatherings.

Hold annual family gatherings to strengthen bonds and pass down traditions. These events should be a blend of old traditions and new experiences. Encourage each generation to share their unique contributions, whether it's a performance, a new family recipe or a special ceremony.

Create a system for documenting and preserving your family's legacy. This can include maintaining a digital archive of photos, videos and documents as well as a physical family history book. Ensure that these records are accessible to all family members.

The library, replete with books from all genres and eras, encourages exploration. It's not just about passing down knowledge but also igniting a thirst for understanding. The legacy is built on encouraging questions and providing the tools to seek answers.

Celebrate family achievements and milestones. Create a hall of achievements or a wall of recognition where accomplishments are proudly displayed. Each generation strives to surpass the last and this room reminds them of the standards set by their predecessors.

Philanthropic Legacy

Engage in philanthropic endeavors together. Discuss and decide on the causes that matter most to your family and actively participate in charity events or volunteer work. This not only leaves a positive impact on the world but reinforces your family's values. It is a reminder that a legacy isn't just about the family but about the impact they have on the world.

CHAPTER TWELVE

BROTHERHOOD

"One's back is vulnerable, unless one has a brother"
- Grettir's Saga

Common sense isn't practical anymore. People know a lot but we don't see it in action. You might have heard the story of a wise old farmer and his four sons.

Once upon a time, in a quiet village, there lived an old farmer. This wise old man had four sons who were constantly at fight with one another. Their ceaseless quarrels weighed heavily on the father's heart. The farmer tried hard to bring unity among them but they would never listen to his advice. He was very worried about their future.

Then, one fateful day, the old farmer's health took a turn for the worse. Realizing that time was not on his side, he decided to make one last attempt to instill unity within his sons. Summoning his four boys, he instructed them to gather a handful of sticks from the nearby surroundings. Eager to please their father, they swiftly collected the sticks and returned to his side.

With a thoughtful look in his eyes, the farmer asked his eldest son to bundle the sticks together tightly. He then challenged his sons to try their utmost to break the bundle apart. Each of the young men took their turn but despite their best efforts, the tightly bound sticks remained unbroken. Then the farmer untied the bundle and gave one stick to each and asked them to break it. Each of them was able to do it easily.

The old farmer, with a smile, spoke to his sons, "Now you see, My dear children. When you stand together, united as one, no one can defeat you.

But if you persist in quarreling amongst yourselves, you will be broken by anyone.".

Now what I am going to talk about is not just about blood brothers. And it's going to be one of the toughest challenges of your life if you try to convert this knowledge into wisdom. Because we live in a divide and rule system. We live in a society where people can't think of more than oneself. Whether you are a man or a woman, use your own judgment. I am going to stick with the term Brotherhood. In the modern world it may be superficially called a mastermind group.

Balance in a man's life hinges on the presence of both the right woman and the right men. Men need a brotherhood. Men need a close-knit circle, where loyalty is the currency, where unity is their strength. They yearn for companions who stand shoulder to shoulder, comrades with whom they wage the battles of life, those who dare to venture into the unknown and who steadfastly guard their backs.

They forge bonds through shared adventures, scaling mountains, conquering waves, and exploring the uncharted. They are the architects of your courage, your sentinels against the storm and the master builders of your character.

Yet, it is in the times of darkness that the true essence of men's brotherhood is revealed. When one of their own stumbles and falls, the others stand as pillars of unwavering support.

The weight of the world is lighter when shared among brothers who stand as one. In the face of adversity, their unity is an unbreakable shield. These bonds are not defined by blood but by choice, by a commitment to be each other's anchors in the stormy seas of life.

Picture a campfire, its warm glow casting dancing shadows on the faces of a group of men, each with a story to tell and a lifetime of memories etched in their hearts. This is the circle of men's brotherhood, where laughter is hearty and silence is profound.

Bond of Brotherhood

You know, it's quite concerning how our system is steering people away from what truly matters in life. We've got this situation where people are becoming increasingly isolated and distracted and let me tell you, that's not a recipe for building strong communities. Isolated and distracted people don't build strong bonds.

Look at our education system. It often feels like it's churning out cogs for the industrial machine. Kids are taught to be productive and their worth is measured solely by their productivity. It's like we're raising a generation of human production units and it's hard to see much purpose beyond that.

What's worse, it seems like the system has little use for old knowledge and wisdom. In fact, it vilifies those who possess such wisdom because, well, a wise person might just disrupt the system itself and the system can't afford that.

And don't even get me started on the soul-crushing work that our entire generation is trapped in. With work taking up so much of our time and energy, there's precious little left for the things that truly matter in life. It's like we're caught in a never-ending cycle of toil and it's leaving us with little room for what really counts.

Brotherhood, my friend, is not an option. It's a necessity. System is so big and powerful, singles can't stand a chance to get out of it. Now, when I speak of brotherhood in this context, I'm not referring to family bonds but rather to the deep, interconnected relationships we build.

Brotherhood is a powerful force for protecting your families. It goes beyond blood ties and extends into the communities and relationships you build throughout your life.

When your family faces a challenge, having a brotherhood to turn to can mean a world of difference. The collective wisdom, experience and resources of the brotherhood can often provide solutions and support that you might not find on your own.

In times of crisis, be it natural disasters, health issues or any unforeseen challenges, a strong brotherhood can be the difference between despair and resilience. Together you can pool resources, provide emotional support and take collective action to overcome the most trying situations.

I'd like to share with you a concept that's often overlooked in the world of business and that is how brotherhood can be a vital catalyst for building and growing businesses together.

In the world of business, resources can be scarce. However within a brotherhood resources can be pooled together. Whether it's financial resources, expertise or industry connections, this collaborative approach can pave the way for expansion and diversification.

Collectively you can explore new markets and ventures that might seem impossible to single one of you. This diversification and expansion become possible due to the combined strength of the brotherhood.

Setbacks are inevitable. Business ventures are never without risks but a close-knit brotherhood can serve as a safety net. When one faces adversity, others can step in to mitigate risks and devise innovative solutions, ensuring the sustained growth of the business.

The exchange of ideas, business secrets and brainstorming together can change the destiny of the business. When brotherhood and all stakeholders are aligned in their aspirations, the potential for growth becomes limitless.

These connections provide a safety net for our emotional wellbeing, helping us navigate the ups and downs of life. It's having a network of people you can confide in, lean on and share your joys and sorrows with. The simple act of talking, sharing and knowing you're not alone can help combat feelings of isolation and depression. Knowing that you have a support system in place can alleviate the burdens that life often throws our way. The sense of belonging and security can act as a shield against the stressors of daily life.

When we have a brotherhood, we are more likely to engage in healthy physical activities. Whether it's exercising together, sports, eating well or seeking challenges, a brotherhood is good for your health.

There is no life in vacuum, There is no happiness in being lonely. Happiness is real when shared. If there is nobody to share your happiness with, it's not. You can deny it for a moment, but in a long life you can't. Man and woman both need their trusted loyal circle, call it brotherhood or anything modern, but that's the necessity.

For all the scientists here, Studies have shown that people with strong social connections tend to live longer. The companionship and emotional nourishment that brotherhood offers can contribute to a longer, happier and healthier life.

In long enough life there will come a tough time, when everyone will betray you, someone will stab you in the back, then only a loyal few will stand with you, that's your brotherhood. They are the only ones. Rest never were. Go, Build Your Brotherhood.

Trust & Loyalty

Vibhishana, the brother of Ravana, is historically known as a traitor because of his choice to betray his own blood, breaking the bonds of loyalty and ultimately dishonoring his brother makes him dishonorable. Based on him there is a popular saying

"घर का भेदी लंका ढाए"

"An insider gets home destroyed."

Brotherhood thrives on trust and loyalty. Trust is the fertile soil in which brotherhood blossoms. Brotherhood thrives on open and honest communication. Encourage conversations that delve beyond surface topics. Share your dreams, fears and aspirations. Ask questions and truly listen to the responses. Take the secrets to the grave.

Show your dedication to the brotherhood through loyalty and commitment. Brothers should be able to confide in one another without fear of betrayal. This trust extends not only to fellow brothers but also to their families, ensuring that everyone is embraced by the protective circle. Your unwavering support during tough times will create unbreakable bonds. Stand by each other, even when the storm clouds gather.

Honor & Respect

"Don't tell me what they said about me. Tell me why they were so comfortable to say it to you." - Denzel Washington

A person of brotherhood should pay those around him his highest level of respect. Disagreements and conflicts are a natural part of any group but respect dictates that they are resolved with patience and mutual understanding.

Disagree Honorably. Just as honoring traditions is part of honor, respecting the customs and rituals of the brotherhood is integral to showing respect. These traditions hold cultural and historical significance, fostering a sense of unity and continuity.

Responsibility & Accountability

Take responsibility for your actions and hold accountable the actions of others. At the core of the responsibilities of brotherhood is the duty to protect one another. This means being a steadfast guardian in times of danger or crisis. Whether it's physical protection, emotional support or financial assistance, a true brother stands ready to shield his comrades from harm.

A true brotherhood is a united front against external threats. This could involve safeguarding the reputation of the group, intervening in conflicts or collectively facing challenges that affect their collective well being. In times of adversity, a brotherhood stands united.

Rituals & Celebrations

In an increasingly fragmented world, where individuals may feel isolated or disconnected, brotherhood rituals offer a sense of belonging and purpose. Create traditions and rituals that honor your unique brotherhood.

Traditions and rituals of brotherhood bring brothers together. When individuals participate in shared activities, they form a collective identity that unites them.

Brotherhood rituals often involve challenges, shared experiences and the building of trust through teamwork. Overcoming these challenges together fosters deep bonds and a sense of camaraderie that is hard to replicate in any other setting. These customs can create opportunities for members to share their experiences, seek guidance and find solace in the knowledge that they are not alone in their struggles.

Mark milestones and achievements with special rituals and ceremonies. This not only honors individual accomplishments but also reinforces the idea that the success of one is the success of all. Through traditions and rituals, brotherhoods strengthen the commitment of their members.

CHAPTER THIRTEEN

RELATIONSHIP

"A great relationship is like a fine wine."

There are two kinds of relationships - selfless and selfish. Modern world just thinks all relationships are selfish and they act that way even in their homes. That is their problem. Let me talk about what I think. Your family relationship is built on love. It's selfless. Your brotherhood, if you have any, is built of people who will fight for you or even die with you. There is a selfless relationship.

Your true friends will not come to you only when they need something. A friend who isn't interested in your life is not a friend. A friend who will not be there, physically or verbally, when you have good times or bad times is not a true friend. There is no difference between the outside world and that friend. But you should still build some good relationships, because together you can shape the world. Things don't happen in the vacuum.

When it comes to cultivating family relationships, I just can't imagine trying to handle it all on my own. It's simply not doable, in my opinion. I mean, singles can barely look after themselves, right?

I'm lucky that my brother is there to manage family relationships, especially when I'm away from my hometown. We live as a family and that's what makes it work. My wife regularly stays in touch with family and relatives when I can't.

Honestly, it's so much easier to manage relationships when you have the support of your family. It's like a team effort and it just works like magic.

To build great relationships, there's no magic trick or technique that can replace one fundamental element: you being a wonderful person to be around. Be wonderful, My friend, that's the secret sauce. Embrace your unique qualities and let your genuine self shine through.

So, if you ever come across someone who's known for having great relationships, take a page out of their book and learn from their example. These incredible folks seem to understand the importance of communication, empathy and trust. They know that it's not just about what you say but how you say it and how well you listen. They're skilled at reading between the lines picking up on the subtleties of human interaction, and responding with kindness and understanding. There are many little things that make you wonderful.

Remember relationships are all about people, not things. People have emotions, things don't. Some people are more sensitive than others. Your choice of words, gentle or harsh, can have a permanent lasting impact. Different people are in different emotional states and moods at different times. You may be angry sometimes but the others aren't. Why spread the negative energies that will bring negative perception of you. Empathy is the key.

Empathy is the ability to understand and share the feelings of others. Let me talk about empathy in friendship and how friendship can be better. It's like walking a mile in their shoes, seeing the world from their perspective and genuinely caring about what they're going through.

Now, empathy is not just about nodding your head and saying, "I understand." It's about really feeling what your friend is feeling. It's about listening with your heart, not just your ears. When your friend is happy, you're genuinely happy for them. When they're hurting, you feel their pain. It's that emotional connection that makes a relationship deeper and more meaningful.

Empathy also means putting yourself in your friend's place when you have a disagreement or conflict. It's about trying to understand where they're coming from even if you don't agree. It doesn't mean you have to give up your own feelings and needs but it does mean you're willing to see their side of the story.

When your friends know that you really "get" them, they feel heard and valued and that's a powerful bond. Listen, understand and support because that's what friendship is for.

Treat others as human beings and not as tools or objects. Treat others as you would like to be treated. Nobody is perfect in everything and treating others with respect takes away nothing. There is no relationship without mutual respect.

Respecting each other's boundaries is a big part of this too. It means understanding and honoring what makes the other person comfortable and what makes him/her uncomfortable. It's about recognizing that everyone has the right to say "no."

Now, let's be clear, mutual respect doesn't mean you'll always agree on everything. Disagreements are a natural part of any relationship and you can disagree respectfully without resorting to insults, put-downs or belittling each other. Both of you will feel safe, valued and supported.

Now you can't have the same kind of relationship with everyone you meet and that's perfectly fine. We're all unique and so are the relationships we form. But what remains constant is who you are as a person. Be the kind of person others want to be around, someone who radiates positivity and authenticity.

It's all about being true to yourself and to others. In an authentic relationship, you don't have to pretend to be someone you're not. You can be your true self with your flaws and all and still be accepted and loved.

Authentic relationships are built on trust and open communication. You can share your thoughts, feelings and concerns without fear of judgment. It's about being there for each other, good or bad. It's a two-way street of understanding and empathy. You listen, you care and you make an effort to truly know the other person. It's about going beyond the surface and getting to know the real person beneath.

Relationships take time. It takes time to establish trust and rapport. If you're a busy person, know that relationships will suffer if you don't invest the time and effort they deserve. No relationship you build will survive if you are too busy to make time for.

Just like a garden, relationships need time to grow and flourish. They need care and attention and they need us to be there from time to time. It's in those shared moments, those conversations, those experiences, that the bonds between people strengthen and deepen.

So, My friend, remember that great relationships are like fine wine; they get better with time. Take the time to be there for the people who matter to you, invest in those connections and watch as they become stronger and more meaningful over the days, months and years.

In any relationship, you can choose between confrontation or cooperation, between being agreeable or disagreeable, between insisting on being right or valuing the relationship itself. The choices you make can shape the course of your relationships.

Let's dive into a fundamental aspect of relationships - how our choices impact the dynamics and quality of our connections with others.

First, we have the choice between confrontation and cooperation in our relationships. Confrontation involves tackling issues head-on, addressing problems and engaging in difficult conversations. On the other hand, cooperation is about working together, finding common ground and seeking solutions as a team. The choice you make here can significantly impact the health of your relationships.

Next, we must consider the balance between being agreeable and disagreeable within a relationship. Being agreeable means going along with the flow, avoiding conflicts and prioritizing harmony. Disagreeable involves expressing differences, offering alternative viewpoints and sometimes engaging in debates. Striking the right balance between these two is important as it can impact how authentic and healthy your relationship is. Mostly, friends are agreeable. If there is constant disagreement and constant confrontation, it won't last long. Theoretically you may think otherwise but that's the reality.

Lastly, we come to the decision of insisting on being right or valuing the relationship itself. When you insist on being right, you prioritize winning arguments, proving your point and asserting your correctness. When you value the relationship itself, you focus on maintaining a positive connection, even if it means letting go of the need to be right all the time. This choice plays a pivotal role in determining whether your relationships are built on mutual respect and understanding or are marred by constant conflicts and power struggles.

The choices you make in these areas will inevitably shape the nature and quality of your relationships. Whether it's confrontation or cooperation, agreeable or disagreeable or insisting on being right vs valuing the relationship itself, think carefully about your choices and how they contribute to the meaningful connections you cherish in your life.

Relationship building is an art and no great art is created without love. Be wonderful, treat people like people and invest the time it takes to nurture meaningful connections.

Call to Action - Family

Provide & Protect

Love & Respect Your Family.

Provide and Protect Your Family.

Plan, Build and Leave a Legacy.

Build Loyal & Strong Brotherhood.

Cultivate True Relationships.

III. World : Power & Control

World is a Myth, It's Made-up.

As we zoom out to the World, it's a bit like looking at a giant puzzle. Power and control play their roles in societies, religions, markets and nations. But guess what? You're not just a piece; you're a key player in the puzzle. Your choices matter in this vast interconnected game.

CHAPTER FOURTEEN

WORLD

They will fool you. Nations will do anything for power. Businesses will do anything for wealth. Religions will do anything for influence. Societies will do anything for status. It's your duty to safeguard yourself and shape the world. Life is a paradox, My friend, you must be a good person and a dangerous person.

Let's begin from the beginning.

Living a holistic life means embracing the multifaceted nature of our existence. It is the art of balancing individual aspirations with the collective welfare of our global civilization. The origin of civilization, war and peace illuminate the interconnectedness of our lives. War, the darkest shadow that has plagued civilization, teaches us the irrevocable cost of conflict. When we study the devastations of history's battlefields, we can no longer underestimate the value of peace. They remind us that our choices have far reaching consequences not only for ourselves but for the world at large.

Civilization

In the heart of the lush, untamed jungle, civilization was but a distant dream. Life was primal, a daily struggle for survival. In the depths of the dense forest, our ancestors roamed, armed with little more than their wits. They foraged for fruits, hunted and sought shelter in caves and makeshift huts woven from vines. It was a world of instinct and adaptability, where every new dawn brought a fresh set of challenges.

Observing the world around them, our ancestors began to experiment with fire, harnessing its power to ward off predators and cook food. This humble flame became the first tool, a symbol of humanity's mastery over nature.

Primitive gestures, grunts and mimicry gave way to more complex forms of expression. Language, as a bridge between minds, allowed communities to share knowledge, stories and dreams. In the glow of a campfire, they painted the walls of their caves with the imagery of their experiences, the world's first art.

Around 10,000 years ago, in different corners of the globe, people discovered the magic of agriculture. They learned to sow seeds and tend to animals. From a meandering river's edge, early farmers learned to cultivate crops, transforming nomadic tribes into settled communities. The soil bore the fruits of their labor and with a surplus of food, they dared to stay put. Villages blossomed, like flowers in spring, marking the first buds of civilization. With the bountiful harvests that followed, surplus food led to the growth of villages, trading networks and a sense of shared identity.

As the villages swelled into towns and towns into cities, a complex dance of society began. Rules and rulers emerged, kings and queens, priests and pharaohs. They orchestrated the grand orchestra of governance, setting the stage for the rise of empires. Across continents, societies traded wares and ideas. The Silk Road, the spice routes and sea voyages intertwined cultures.

On the pages of history, powerful empires left their indelible marks. The Romans conquered vast territories and the Mongols galloped across continents like a tempest.

Empires rose and empires fell, shaping the course of civilization.

Then, in the heart of Europe, the Renaissance ignited like a phoenix from the ashes. Art, science and philosophy flourished, breathing new life into the human spirit. Enlightenment illuminated minds, fostering ideals of liberty, reason and progress.

The evolution of civilization took a leap forward as they discovered the secrets of metalworking, learned to navigate the seas and built towering structures that reached for the skies.

But the true revolution was yet to come - the Industrial Revolution. It unleashed the power of machines, churning out progress in steel and steam. Factories, railways and inventions reshaped societies, steering them from fields to factories. The Industrial Revolution was a turning point in history, marked by the transition from agrarian and handcraft based economies to industrialized and mechanized societies.

It began in the late 18th century with the mechanization of textile production and the widespread use of steam power and it extended into the 19th century. Key developments included the construction of factories, the expansion of transportation networks and the growth of urban centers.

This revolution revolutionized manufacturing processes, allowing for mass production, which, in turn, led to increased productivity and economic growth. The Industrial Revolution also brought about significant social and demographic changes as people migrated to cities and it laid the foundation for modern capitalism.

And as the wheels of time continued to turn, another revolution quietly stirred—the Internet Revolution also known as the Information Age, began in the late 20th century with the advent of the World Wide Web and the expansion of the internet. This revolution has fundamentally transformed the way we communicate, access information, conduct business and connect with one another. The internet has enabled instant global communication, the democratization of knowledge and the rise of e-commerce, social media and online education. It has also catalyzed a new era of globalization, reshaping economies, politics and culture.

It's a journey from simple beginnings to the complex and interconnected world we live in today. Today, in the vibrant present, we dwell in an intricate web of nations and technologies. Yet, in the depth of our collective memory, the spirit of that primal wilderness still echoes - a reminder of where we began and the untamed roots that continue to shape our civilization today.

War

In today's world, we often don't realize how harsh and brutal wars can be. This is because we are surrounded by technology, social media and a constant flow of information. These things make it seem like the suffering caused by wars is far away and not so real.

The problems of the world are shown to us as small pictures and quick news stories. They are quickly replaced by funny videos and memes. It's as if our online world and the real world have become mixed up, so we forget about the pain of war. Wars become just numbers and politics and we forget about the real people who are hurt by them.

Our schools teach us about history but not always about the harsh parts of it. They keep the bad things away from us and we don't learn much about what wars are really like. So we grow up not knowing much about how tough wars can be.

War is a dark chapter in human history, a period of despair, destruction and sorrow. And it repeats, again and again and again.

War often begins with a surprise, the deafening roar of artillery or the occupation of disputed territories. The world listens as the storm clouds gather and thunder clashes with lightning on the horizon.

Conflict zones emerge and nations start mobilizing their forces. Troops, tanks and fighter jets rumble into life and the world feels the shudder of a world at war.

The conflict zones become crucibles of chaos, where the machinery of war grinds on relentlessly. Cities tremble under the weight of artillery and the ground bears witness to the shedding of blood and tears.

Economies are disrupted as nations divert vast resources into the war effort. Inflation surges, trade falters and the stability of currencies quivers under the immense strain.

Civilians become the unintended actors in a play of chaos and conflict. Their lives, once marked by simplicity, are thrust onto a stage they never wished to tread.

Fear, like a ghostly specter, haunts the daily lives of people. Every distant explosion, every overhead roar of fighter jets, sends shivers down their spines. The routine sounds of life are drowned out by the drumbeat of artillery.

In the times of war, freedom, that cherished bird of liberty, finds its wings clipped.

State-sponsored propaganda churns out a discordant narrative. Truth becomes a casualty, replaced by half-truths and distortions. The lines between fact and fiction blur and freedom of thought is challenged.

Personal choices are limited as food, goods and resources are distributed by government decree. What one eats, wears and consumes is no longer a matter of personal choice.

Citizens may find themselves compelled into forced labor, building the infrastructure of war or toiling for the benefit of the state. The ability to choose one's vocation evaporates.

The fear of arbitrary arrests looms. Individuals can be detained without trial and the threat of incarceration hangs over even casual dissent. The once open forums for debate and expression wither.

Borders tighten and the ability to move freely is curtailed. Travel becomes a bureaucratic ordeal and passports bear the weight of permits. The world once an open book becomes a series of locked doors.

War begets a humanitarian crisis. Displaced families wander, seeking refuge while others are trapped in the crossfire. Food, water and medical supplies become scarce and the world hears the cries of those who suffer.

For some, the only choice is to flee, leaving behind the lives they've known. Roads become rivers of humanity and distant lands offer uncertain refuge. Displacement becomes a necessity, where families carry the weight of their past, uncertain of what the future holds.

The legacy of war is indelible. It leaves scars in the minds and hearts of those who survived forever, both soldiers and civilians.

In today's busy world with screens all around us, the brutality of wars is hidden. We need to look past the distractions, learn the stories that aren't often told and face the hard truths. Only then can we break free from the fake world that keeps us from seeing the painful reality of wars and work toward a world without them.

Civilization's journey through history has been marked by the trials and tribulations of war, with some of the biggest conflicts serving as defining moments in our survival.

Two colossal wars in the 20th century, known as World War I and World War II, shook the foundations of civilization. These wars were so massive that they involved many nations from around the world. Millions of lives were lost and entire cities were reduced to ruins.

World War I, which began in 1914, was a war unlike any other, with new weapons and technologies that caused unprecedented destruction. It reshaped borders and led to the redrawing of maps.

However, World War II, which started in 1939, was even more devastating. It included the Holocaust, a horrific genocide that claimed the lives of millions. But in the aftermath of this war, the world united once more to establish the United Nations, a global organization aimed at preventing future wars and promoting peace and cooperation.

Following World War II, the world entered a new era marked by tension and rivalry between the United States and the Soviet Union, known as the Cold War. While it wasn't a hot, full-scale war, it was a time of great unease and the constant threat of nuclear conflict. Despite the fear of mutually assured destruction, humanity survived this prolonged period of global tension.

Throughout history, there have been numerous other major wars and conflicts, such as the American Civil War, the Korean War, Bangladesh Liberation War, Gulf War, Balkan Wars, Rwandan Genocide, Kosovo War, Chechen War, Iraq War, Afghanistan War, Libyan Civil War, South Sudan Civil War, Syrian Civil War, Yemeni Civil War,Israel-Gaza conflict, Ukraine War, Israel-Hamas War. The list is endless.

War is the stark truth, where your very essence is no longer your own. When the clamor of war encircles you, you become an instrument of the state, a pawn in the grand game. It's time to awaken to this reality.

It's the decisions of people in power which decides the destiny of the masses. Decisions of leaders have consequences for their people.

Action Items: *Do your holistic research on decisions of leaders and their consequences in Ukraine - Russia War and Israel-Hamas Conflict.*

Peace

Humanity's greatest triumphs lie not in the victories of war but in the enduring legacy of peace. The true power of mankind is not in the ability to destroy but in the capacity to build, to heal and to dream.

Schools and universities are vibrant sanctuaries of knowledge, nurturing curious minds and fostering a deep sense of understanding and appreciation for the world's diverse cultures and perspectives. Every child, regardless of their background, has access to quality education, unlocking the potential for untold discoveries and breakthroughs.

Economic prosperity flourishes like never before as resources once squandered on war machines are redirected toward infrastructure, education and healthcare. Innovation and creativity thrive as the human intellect is unburdened by the shadows of war allowing for the birth of new technologies and the exploration of uncharted frontiers. Scientists explore the cosmos while engineers craft solutions to pressing global challenges.

In this era of peace, art and culture find their truest expression, reflecting the depths of the human soul. Writers craft eloquent prose and poetry, Poets pen verses that sing of love and unity. Artists paint canvases that breathe with the colors of harmony. Musicians compose symphonies that resonate with the sweet notes of tranquility. Art transcends boundaries, speaking a universal language of emotion and empathy reminding humanity of its shared dreams and aspirations.

People from different backgrounds and cultures come together to share in the richness of their diversity realizing that unity is the catalyst for progress. A sense of global citizenship takes root and international collaboration becomes the cornerstone of solving the world's most pressing issues from poverty eradication to environmental conservation.

Individuals are free to pursue their passions and dreams unburdened by the heavy armor of conflict. Communities embrace the values of empathy and social justice ensuring that no one is left behind in the pursuit of happiness.

It is a time when the bonds of unity, progress and compassion converge to create a world where the potential of each individual is celebrated and the collective endeavor of humanity knows no bounds.

In the wisdom of our past, we find the guidance to build a more compassionate, equitable and sustainable future. By learning from the mistakes and successes of our predecessors we can navigate the complexities of the modern world with a profound sense of purpose. We become not only the beneficiaries of our heritage but the stewards of the legacy we leave for generations to come. Things don't always unfold as idealistically as we hope. Now tell me you want war or peace?

CHAPTER FIFTEEN

SOCIETIES

Forget for a moment what society is. How would you define an ideal society?

It is a place where individuals of all backgrounds and beliefs come together, each carrying their own unique story and perspective.

It is a place where the wisdom of elders dances with the exuberance of youth and where innovative ideas collide with traditions.

It is a place where challenges and conflicts arise, where the struggle for a more equitable and compassionate world is a constant refrain. It is a place where inequalities lurk in the corners where the dissonance of prejudice and injustice can disrupt the harmonious life.

It's a place for heroes and villains, dreamers and realists, rebels and conformists. Each plays their role contributing to the ongoing drama of society.

It is a place where innovation sparks revolutions, where art inspires change and where the human spirit endures through the ages.

It's a story of love and loss, hope and despair, progress and setbacks.

Game of Status

Remember Leaders don't complain, They shape the Society.

In the drama of society, status is the costume that we wear, the character we portray and the role we play.

Status is like a radiant star, casting its glow on those who have ascended the ranks of power, wealth and influence. These individuals become the protagonists of the societal drama, admired and sometimes even envied for their achievements.

Status can become a source of inspiration or a weighty burden. It can be used to elevate others, lending a voice to those in need and driving positive change. But it can also become a prison, where expectations and judgments confine individuals, where the glare of the spotlight can be blinding.

Status is not merely a reflection of our external achievements but also a mirror to our internal values and principles. It speaks to the choices we make, the causes we champion and the legacy we hope to leave behind.

Consider it a reminder that in the drama of society we all play our roles and each character contributes to the ongoing drama.

You can become a force for positive change and a source of inspiration for a better society. Change begins with self.

Imagine yourself as that role model. Your actions speak louder than your words. You lead by example, embodying the values and principles you hold dear. You radiate authenticity, showing the world that you are unapologetically yourself. You embrace your flaws and vulnerabilities, for it's in these imperfections that your humanity shines most brightly. You understand that perfection is an illusion but honesty and humility are real and relatable.

You are an advocate for inclusivity and diversity, championing the idea that our differences are what make us stronger. Your embrace of various perspectives and cultures creates an environment where everyone feels welcome, valued and heard.

You're a relentless pursuer of knowledge and personal growth. Your intellectual curiosity is infectious, igniting a flame of learning in others, reminding them that they can constantly expand their horizons.

Through your creative endeavors, you have the power to ignite change and shape a society that values self expression, diversity and inclusion. Your art can inspire others to join you in making a difference. Your work can bridge the gap between different cultures, backgrounds and beliefs. It can ignite conversations, promote tolerance and unite people.

As a self aware or spiritual person, you can be a role model by radiating inner peace and resilience. Your calm demeanor, even in the face of life's storms, can inspire others to seek inner harmony and find strength in challenging times. You can inspire society to look inward, fostering a culture of mindfulness, compassion and interconnectedness.

Traps of Society

Every society has its traps but I am going to talk about where I am from.

It's quite fascinating to see how Indian society is caught up in this ever-rising trend of showoffs, extravagant ceremonies and materialism. I mean, it's like this wave of wanting to outdo each other has just engulfed us all.

We've all witnessed it, right? The grand, over-the-top weddings that sometimes leave you wondering if they're more about showcasing wealth than celebrating love. The pressure to keep up with the neighbors, friends and even strangers leads people to spend way beyond their means.

The obsession with brand names, flashy cars and designer clothes seems to be on the rise. It's as if our worth is measured by what we own, rather than who we are as individuals. Materialism, it's everywhere you look.

This trend, it's not only putting a strain on people's finances but also on their mental and emotional well-being. The constant need to prove oneself and maintain appearances can be exhausting.

I think, as a society, we should reflect on where these trends are leading us. Are we losing sight of what truly matters in life? It's important to remember that genuine happiness often lies in simpler things – in the love of our family, the warmth of our friendships and the contentment of a meaningful life.

Social Issues

When I talk about society, I am talking as much about you and me as much about people who live in society. Directly or indirectly, It has everything to do with us. The issues I'm going to address here concern us and I am writing this to shed light on how the world can sometimes deceive us. There are a lot of good things but it's the problems that need the solution. There are two kinds of blind people in this world, who can't see and who won't see. It's in our best interest to be aware and be informed. Let's begin with cultural issues.

Culture

A great culture invites us to question, experiment and create without fear of judgment or the restrictions of conformity. It empowers us to celebrate diversity, individuality and the ever-evolving nature of human thought and creativity.

So, let us remember that in the realm of modernism, freedom of mind is the guiding principle. It's not about being enslaved by the dictates of taste but rather about unleashing the full potential of our imagination and embracing the richness of human diversity.

Let's talk about a topic that concerns the very fabric of our society - the corrosion of our culture and its potential descent into moral decay.

One concerning trend is the declining respect for knowledge. In a world awash with information, we often find knowledge overlooked or even dismissed. This devaluation of wisdom can lead to ignorance and a loss of our moral compass.

Identity too has been misconstrued with many deriving their sense of self worth solely from their work. In doing so, we risk losing sight of our intrinsic value as human beings, reduced to mere economic units.

In an era marked by ruthless selfishness, it's become commonplace to prioritize personal gain without considering the cost to others. This self-centered attitude has the potential to erode the bonds that hold our society together.

No youth is immune to this cultural corrosion. They can be exposed to hatred and harmful ambitions through distorted historical narratives and misrepresentations of other races. This breeds unfavorable sentiments and poisons the very essence of our shared humanity.

We've witnessed the discrediting of noble ideals that were born from the lives of great individuals. In their place children may be taught contempt for others and individuals may cheat others for the sake of vulgar profits.

The use of phrases like "Business is Business" and "Politics is Politics" can strip these facets of life of their humanity, turning them into cold, calculated endeavors. We must remember that business and politics are deeply human endeavors and they should be conducted with respect for the richness of self-expression and the depth of self-control.

Let us rekindle the richness of self-expression and the depth of self-control and strive for a society that values not just success but also empathy and human connection.

Power

We're on a treacherous path in today's world. What we see is a relentless chase for power and wealth and it's coming at the expense of our collective well-being. This pursuit of dominance and control is overshadowing the value of humanity itself. We find ourselves in a society where the acquisition of power is held above all else and it's beginning to take its toll on the very essence of who we are.

This quest for power is showing its face in various ways from the colossal growth of corporations to the rise of authoritarian governments. It's driven by ambition and greed and it's at times at the cost of individual freedoms and human welfare. The power structures that have emerged are crushing the very spirit of humanity and pushing people into a never ending cycle of subservience.

Look at the behavior of corporations. Many of them accumulate immense wealth and influence but prioritize maintaining their status even if it means exploiting their workforce and ignoring ethical concerns. Employees become mere cogs in the machine, subjected to relentless demands for the sake of profit with their well-being sacrificed on the altar of financial supremacy.

Governments and public leaders are prioritizing control and authority over the welfare of their citizens, suppressing dissent and infringing upon individual rights in the name of national interests. This lust for power results in a society where the voices of the people are stifled, their freedoms restricted and their spirit dampened.

The relentless ambition and greed in the pursuit of power have led us to a crossroads where the value of human life is overshadowed by the quest for dominance. It's a path that leads to the erosion of the human spirit.

True power isn't about controlling others; it's about lifting each other up, fostering a sense of belonging and creating a world where the human spirit can flourish. It requires leaders who are driven not solely by ambition and greed but by a genuine commitment to the welfare of their constituents. We need to reevaluate our societal values and build systems that prioritize the betterment of humanity.

Status

We live in a time when power, wealth and fame are given more respect and importance than the very core of human values and our humanity. We're moving towards a world where the superficial display of material possessions is celebrated while the nurturing of our inner selves is slowly fading away.

This growing emphasis on the external, the display of opulence and the pursuit of extravagance is rampant, be it in our clothing, our desire for luxury, the size of our cars or the grandeur of our villas. It's as if we've placed a higher premium on what we own rather than who we are. The essence of humanity is being overshadowed by the relentless pursuit of material possessions.

We find ourselves valuing things over people. The worth of a person seems to be judged by the brands they wear, the cars they drive and the size of their homes. We've somehow allowed the pursuit of status to take precedence over the deeper, more meaningful aspects of our existence, such as empathy and human connection.

Let's celebrate not just what we possess but who we are inside. It's in nurturing our inner well-being, our shared human values and our connections with one another that we can find the fulfillment and richness that no material possession can ever replace.

Scams and Frauds

Let's not forget the pervasive issue that affects our society, the insidious presence of scams and frauds. It's a problem that often goes unnoticed but can have far-reaching consequences.

At the heart of these scams are con men who prey on our vulnerabilities, capitalizing on human weaknesses like greed, selfishness and the allure of easy money. These individuals craft ruthless plans that exploit trust and manipulate individuals into believing they're on the path to prosperity.

Scams come in many forms, from the more obvious easy money-making schemes to those that cloak themselves with reputable tournament sponsorships and the façade of legitimacy. Behind the shiny buildings and smiling faces, dark secrets lurk, waiting to be unveiled.

In recent times, the rise of online scams and frauds has become particularly concerning. From financial fraud and scams to gambling to fantasy sports to internet blackmail and even matrimonial fraud, the web has become a breeding ground for these deceitful practices.

The impact of these scams and frauds cannot be understated. They are parasitic, leeching away trust, financial security and peace of mind from society. Our leaders and laws reveal themselves to be weak and ill-prepared to combat this growing menace.

We need stronger laws, stricter regulations and better enforcement to protect our citizens. But, ultimately, it's our collective responsibility to educate ourselves and those around us fostering a culture of awareness and resilience against scams and frauds.

Media

What role is the media playing in shaping our society? We're witnessing how the media can be used to manipulate, through the insidious tools of propaganda, the selective presentation of facts, half-truths and even the spread of fake news.

Propaganda is a powerful tool that can be used to influence public opinion, without the audience realizing it.

Whether it's in the form of political bias, hidden agendas or sensationalism, media manipulation has the potential to reshape our beliefs and perceptions.

The selective presentation of facts and bending the truth can lead to a distorted view of reality. It's as though we're being presented with a fragmented puzzle with pieces deliberately missing. This can have a significant impact on our understanding of events and issues.

Half-truths are particularly insidious because they contain elements of truth, making them all the more convincing. By blending facts with fiction, half-truths can lead us down a slippery slope of misinformation and we often don't see the full picture.

The most concerning is the spread of fake news which is deliberately created to deceive and mislead. The power of fake news lies in its ability to stir emotions, create divisions and undermine trust in credible sources of information.

Media manipulation can have far-reaching consequences. It can fuel polarization, sow discord and even influence elections and policies. In a world where the line between fact and fiction is increasingly blurred, it's essential for us to approach information critically and for media outlets to uphold the principles of truth, accuracy and impartiality.

Slavery

A matter of great concern in our society today is the increasing control that corporations exercise over the lives of their employees. It's not just about where you work and your work hours; it goes much deeper.

Corporations have extended their reach to dictate not only when employees arrive and leave but also how they behave, what they share and even what they say. The liberty of the soul seems to be at stake with employees feeling compelled to conform not only during working hours but also outside of them. The need to change oneself to align with the corporate image and values is becoming a norm.

This situation forces individuals to mold themselves to be more attractive to potential employers, effectively suppressing their authenticity. The question that arises is, if employees cannot enjoy the freedom of their thoughts and corporations wield such control over the markets, how can our society truly be considered free?

As corporations continue to tighten their hold on markets, people's choices for work are becoming limited and the prospect of escaping this system is diminishing. The idea of a more equitable partnership-based system rather than traditional employment is being pushed to the margins because it doesn't serve those in power.

The window of opportunity for change seems to be closing. It's a form of modern slavery that goes beyond physical slavery and it's of utmost importance that we consider how we can safeguard our individual freedoms and reclaim a society where people are not just cogs in the corporate machinery but truly free to express themselves and make choices that align with their values and aspirations.

To be honest we never got out of slavery, it just transformed itself in shape and size so big that it seems like a norm and how can norm be a form of slavery. This time it's bigger and invisible to those who want to stay blind.

Education

What is the education system doing? - the suppression of free thinking with the emphasis on conformity. The current system trains kids to work for the powerful rather than empowering them to think for themselves. The focus on obedience and adherence to the status quo can hinder their ability to question, challenge and innovate.

The focus is on achieving high test scores rather than fostering intellectual curiosity and problem-solving abilities. Children are taught to be achievement-oriented, striving for grades and accomplishments rather than understanding the profound purpose of education itself. Education should not be merely about accumulating knowledge; it's about learning how to think and how to become wise individuals.

The purpose of education should be to nurture young minds, enabling them to think independently and make informed decisions. There is a need for a shift in our educational systems towards fostering creativity, critical thinking and wisdom, equipping children to thrive as free thinkers in an ever-evolving world.

But that's dangerous for powerful people. It's not in their interest to raise a population full of wise men and women. Because then they can't control, can't exploit. Only the people can do that while they still can.

Politics

In a democracy, politicians are elected to represent and serve the best interests of their people. But we all know that for most politicians the pursuit of power and personal gain are priority over genuine public service.

All politicians use rhetoric that suggests they're champions of the people, vowing to bring about positive change and improvements. But in reality their primary objective may be to secure and consolidate their own power. This manipulation often involves playing on the hopes and fears of the public, promising solutions that seem too good to be true. Sadly, once in office, these politicians prioritize their own agendas and interests, leaving the promises made during their campaigns unfulfilled.

Corruption undermines the very foundation of trust in our government institutions. The consequences of corruption extend beyond just a loss of trust. It siphons public resources away from essential services like education, healthcare and infrastructure, leaving our communities underserved and hindered in their development. Corruption also distorts the decision-making process, as policies and laws may be influenced by financial gain rather than the best interests of the public. This compromises the very ideals of justice and fairness.

We can use politics as a powerful tool for social good by actively participating, staying informed, advocating for our beliefs, fostering cooperation and promoting transparency and accountability. By working together, we can shape a more just and equitable society through the political process.

We must engage actively in the political process and even aspire to be politicians. Because that's how we change the system. In a healthy democracy, politicians are meant to be servants of the people, not masters driven by personal ambition.

Science

While science undoubtedly provides us with valuable insights and knowledge, relying solely on it for our life philosophies can lead to a hollow and superficial life.

Science, as a discipline, deals with facts, measurements and empirical evidence. It's a powerful tool for understanding the natural world and it has brought us remarkable advancements. However, life itself is a complex creation of emotions, experiences and intangible qualities that extend far beyond what science can quantify.

When we base our life philosophies solely on scientific principles, we risk overlooking the profound aspects of our existence. It can lead to a life that feels somewhat lifeless, devoid of the deeper meaning and purpose that comes from our emotions, our relationships and our individual journeys.

Life is not a series of equations or experiments; it's a deeply personal and subjective experience. It's about love, inspiration, happiness and aspirations. These are aspects of life that cannot be measured under a microscope or subjected to scientific analysis.

That's not to say that science and life philosophies are incompatible; they can complement each other beautifully. We should embrace the knowledge and understanding that science provides but we must also recognize the limitations of a purely scientific worldview.

In this pursuit of a rich and meaningful life we need a balance between the objective and the subjective, between science and the intangible qualities that make our existence profoundly human. Our life philosophies should be a blend of rationality and emotion, of reason and passion, to truly embrace the depth and beauty of the human experience.

Architectures

The aesthetics of modern architecture fall short of the timeless beauty that we see in ancient structures. Contemporary buildings seem to have neglected the very essence of beauty in their design.

In contrast to the artistic and intricate designs of ancient architecture, we often find today's buildings characterized by stark, boxy shapes and flat, unadorned wall surfaces. It's as though we've become trapped within these square, lifeless structures, devoid of the captivating allure that we find in historic architectural marvels.

The question we must ask is whether we're willing to compromise the importance of beauty in the built environment. While functionality and efficiency are essential, so too is the visual harmony and inspiration that architecture can provide. The buildings we inhabit have the power to influence our mood, creativity and overall well-being. It's crucial that we don't neglect the role of beauty in this equation.

In our pursuit of modernity and convenience, let us not forget the significance of architectural beauty. Strive to create spaces that not only serve their intended purpose but also uplift the human spirit through the timeless magic of aesthetics. Our surroundings play a significant role in shaping our lives and the inclusion of beauty in our architectural designs can enrich our daily experiences and inspire future generations.

CHAPTER SIXTEEN

RELIGIONS

"The greatest religion is to be true to your own nature. Have faith in yourselves." - Swami Vivekanand

Religion has been a source of both great enlightenment and bitter division. Throughout history it has been a double-edged sword capable of inspiring both acts of immense compassion and appalling cruelty. Religion is a reflection of humanity's virtues and vices, our capacity for love and our susceptibility to fear. Faith in religion comes with its shadows and complexities.

It provides answers to life's profound questions and solace in times of despair. It is a lighthouse guiding us through the turbulent seas of existence, offering hope and redemption to those who seek it.

The same scriptures that preach love and harmony have, at times, been wielded as weapons of exclusion and hatred. In the name of faith, wars have been waged and atrocities committed, all fueled by the fervor of religious zealotry. It has been a catalyst for bloodshed, sowing the seeds of intolerance and conflict.

Religion often bears the weight of the human condition. It can provide the foundation for justice and social change, inspiring individuals to champion the causes of the marginalized and oppressed. It calls for the protection of life, the pursuit of knowledge and the alleviation of suffering urging us to strive for a better world.

Simultaneously it can be the crucible of dogma, constraining the free spirit and chaining it to rigid doctrines. It can resist progress, deter scientific inquiry and foster prejudice against those who do not share its tenets. The blade of religion when wielded with a heavy hand can cut down the very freedoms it purports to protect.

As you follow faith, you must tread carefully recognizing the capacity for both good and ill that you narrate from the sacred texts and rituals. It can be a tool for unity, understanding and compassion or a weapon of division, hatred and intolerance.

Religion, once a personal journey into the divine, has transformed into a vast and intricate organization. Religious leaders once humble guides on the path to spiritual enlightenment, now find themselves overseeing vast congregations. What began as a quest for the sacred has become a tool of control. They are no longer just houses of worship but also vast empires of faith with budgets, laws and even political influence. The ideals of compassion, forgiveness and love sometimes coexist with issues of wealth, hierarchy and control.

Game of Influence

Remember God doesn't belong to any religion.

Religion plays both the role of a guide and a tool of manipulation.

Religious influence is found in the sacred texts and scriptures, where timeless wisdom and moral guidance are imparted to generations. These words are the keystones of belief, shaping the values, rituals and ethics of followers.

Imagine a world where beliefs and doctrines are the reins by which societies are steered, where the pulpit becomes a pedestal of power and where the faithful are both devout followers and unwitting pawns in the grand game of control.

Religion with its potent brew of mythology, morality and mysticism, has always held the allure of authority. It presents a narrative of divine purpose, a transcendent order and the promise of eternal rewards. As such, it can be a powerful tool for those who seek to shape or manipulate society.

Historically rulers have often claimed their authority as a divine mandate, intertwining their reign with religious dogma. A clever manipulation of this belief can turn the public into loyal devotees, who accept their ruler's dominion as a manifestation of God's will. The connection between earthly and heavenly authority becomes a potent tool for control.

Religion can be employed to keep society in check through the fear of divine retribution. A clergy that wields the power to punish or condemn can stifle dissent and enforce conformity. Those who question the established order risk the wrath of the divine, a psychological mechanism that can instill obedience and discourage rebellion.

In times of hardship and uncertainty, religion offers solace. The promise of a better afterlife can pacify those enduring suffering, reducing their inclination to challenge the societal structures that might be causing their pain. Faith can act as an opiate, numbing the suffering of the oppressed and facilitating societal control.

Religion often draws lines between those who belong and those who don't, fostering an "us vs them" mentality. By defining the "other" as heretics or infidels, religious leaders can manipulate their followers into viewing outsiders with suspicion and hostility, thereby consolidating control over their own flock.

Rituals and symbols are powerful tools for control. These can serve as a unifying force within a society, establishing a shared identity and fostering a sense of belonging. Those who deviate from these rituals may be ostracized or labeled as outsiders, effectively controlling the behavior and beliefs of the population.

Religious institutions often have a monopoly on knowledge and education. By controlling what is taught, they can shape the worldview of their followers. This control over knowledge extends to censorship and suppression, ensuring that dissenting voices are silenced or discredited.

Religion under right leaders can be a force for good through community. Houses of worship, churches, mosques or temples are hubs for social interaction. They bring people together, fostering a sense of belonging and unity. This sense of community can lead to collective efforts to address social issues and help those in need.

Some religious institutions also engage in charitable activities. From food drives to clothing donations to disaster relief efforts, religious groups have a long history of providing assistance to those who are less fortunate. Their dedication to serving the vulnerable and promoting social justice is an example of the positive impact of religion.

Religion that divides people is a religion which is under control of corrupt leaders. In that case you should take your own spiritual journey, read scriptures yourself and take messages in the right context to have a true understanding of religion. Applying a message from one context into another is a recipe for disaster.

Extremism of Religion

It's really heart-wrenching to see how some countries are torn apart by extremist religious ideologies and terrorism. If you live in an environment where extremist ideology is spreading, you may be in great trouble any day. Here is why. This is a problem that has plagued various parts of the world and I can give you some examples to illustrate just how devastating it can be.

One striking example is Afghanistan. For decades Afghanistan has been deeply affected by extremist groups like the Taliban. Their strict interpretation of religious law has led to severe human rights violations and instability in the region. The country has suffered from war, violence and the suppression of basic freedoms.

Another example is the rise of ISIS, an extremist group that exploited religious differences, causing immense destruction in their countries. Their acts of terror not only targeted civilians but also contributed to sectarian violence and political instability.

In Nigeria, Boko Haram is another painful example. This extremist group has carried out numerous attacks, abduction and spreading fear through their violent actions, all in the name of a twisted interpretation of religion.

And let's not forget about Syria. The Syrian Civil War has been fueled by various extremist elements, including ISIS, which has resulted in countless deaths, a refugee crisis and unimaginable suffering for the Syrian people.

These examples are just a snapshot of the broader issue of how extremist religious ideologies and terrorism can wreak havoc on countries and their populations.

Your Journey

People run religion and people get corrupted. But that doesn't make religion and spirituality a bad thing. The impact of spiritual work is extraordinary. Most people do nothing but complain as if they have no duty but to be served by a perfect society, a perfect religion and a perfect nation. Everybody shapes society and it's future.

Spiritual Leaders

Spiritual leaders shape society by fostering moral values, promoting unity, advocating for justice, inspiring personal growth and encouraging acts of kindness. Their influence extends beyond their immediate followers and can touch the hearts and minds of people across the world, making our society a more compassionate and just place to live.

They are often the custodians of moral and ethical principles. These values are the foundation of a harmonious and just society and spiritual leaders help instill them in the hearts and minds of their followers.

Spiritual leaders also foster a sense of unity and belonging within their communities. They create spaces for people to come together, connect and find support in times of joy and sorrow. In a world often divided by differences, spiritual leaders can bridge gaps and promote understanding among diverse groups.

Many spiritual leaders have been at the forefront of movements that seek to alleviate poverty, combat discrimination and promote equality. Their moral authority can be a powerful catalyst for addressing societal issues and driving positive transformation.

They are instrumental in promoting the well-being of society. They offer guidance on how to find inner peace, deal with life's challenges and lead a more meaningful existence. This contributes to a healthier and happier society.

They conduct charity and community services. Their teachings often emphasize the importance of helping others and their followers frequently engage in philanthropic efforts that benefit the less fortunate and contribute to the betterment of society as a whole.

Volunteers

Practically nothing unites people like religion. With this unity, people can do community services for social good. Many religious organizations are involved in international relief efforts, providing aid to those affected by disasters, conflict and poverty. This not only helps people in need but also enhances a nation's morale and reputation on the global stage.

Religious volunteers are often at the forefront of efforts to address societal issues. They engage in activities like feeding the hungry, providing shelter to the homeless and caring for the sick. This hands-on approach to social problems can lead to tangible improvements in the lives of those they serve. The dedication and service by volunteering can help create a more compassionate, inclusive and caring society for all.

Historically it was religion which brought people together for volunteer work, Modern influencers are also directing their followers for social good. Volunteer work is like a driving force for positive change. When people dedicate their time to causes they are passionate about, they can address pressing social issues, support those in need and contribute to the betterment of our society. Whether it's feeding the hungry, tutoring students, caring for the elderly or cleaning up the environment, these selfless acts make a tangible difference.

There is a profound beauty in looking beyond "What's in it for me?" This kind of selflessness can't be learned in a classroom or from a textbook; it can only be experienced through the act of service.

CHAPTER SEVENTEEN

MARKETS

It is a drama of innovation, competition and human ambition where the script is written in the currency of supply and demand.

The businesses and markets drama is not just about profit and loss, it is a reflection of human ingenuity and ambition. It is a testament to our capacity to adapt and evolve. It is a tale of risk and reward, of dreams realized and ambitions achieved.

Competition can be fierce and unforgiving. Just as in a drama they may encounter unexpected twists, economic downturns and shifting consumer preferences. Businesses must adapt, improvise and innovate to capture the spotlight.

It's a game of Investors and traders navigating the twists and turns of the markets, the euphoria of a bull market where optimism soars and the gloom of a bear market where pessimism prevails. It is a place where fortunes can be made or lost in the blink of an eye.

Advertising and marketing are the scripts, weaving a narrative that captivates the imagination and stirs desire.

Game of Wealth

Remember a lot depends on Wealth and a lot is controlled by Wealth.

We live in a world where the pursuit of wealth has become an all-consuming obsession for some, transcending ethical boundaries and moral constraints.

Some capitalists driven by a relentless thirst for riches view the labor of individuals as a mere means to an end. In their ceaseless quest for profit, they exploit the labor force, treating workers as expendable cogs in the machinery of capitalism, squeezing every drop of effort, creativity and time from them.

These exploiters are like puppeteers, pulling the strings of their workers, coercing them to labor long hours for meager wages, all the while reaping the lion's share of the spoils. The profit margins expand, dividends grow fatter and executive bonuses swell, all while the exploited toil in the shadows of inequity.

As capitalists ruthlessly pursue wealth, they often perpetuate socioeconomic disparities. The most vulnerable among us, the working-class heroes, bear the brunt of this exploitation, trapped in cycles of poverty and injustice, with limited access to education, healthcare or opportunities for upward mobility. This predatory aspect of capitalism leaves scars on individuals and communities where the promise of prosperity remains elusive and the wealth gap widens into a gaping chasm.

Many businesses and entrepreneurs prioritize fair wages, workers rights and ethical business practices. They endeavor to create a symbiotic relationship with their workforce, fostering an environment where both prosperity and well-being can coexist.

The path society chooses to follow within this system will determine whether capitalism becomes a force for good or a perpetuator of inequality, where the pursuit of riches comes at the cost of human dignity and well-being. A society that seeks to harness capitalism's potential for innovation, prosperity and progress must also be vigilant in ensuring that no one is sacrificed at the altar of wealth.

Businesses like any system must evolve, with regulations and ethical considerations curbing exploitation and promoting human wellbeing.

The need to make wealth is also a force for societal progress. It stimulates economies, fuels innovation and drives technological advancements. It encourages individuals to invest in education, explore uncharted territories and create opportunities for others. In this way, the pursuit of wealth becomes a collective endeavor, lifting entire communities to higher standards of living.

Wealth creation is about supplying what society demands. Using Your creative and critical thinking to find new avenues for revenue and growth through sound financial choices. Wealth creation isn't just about knowledge; it's also a dance of risk and reward. This is a field you must master through both knowledge and practice.

Exploitations by Market

Almost all businesses are taking advantage of the public by promoting a culture of consumerism, imposing soul-sucking work conditions and leading people down a path that can feel like a form of modern-day slavery through quick loans and credit cards.

These businesses often bombard the public with advertisements that create this insatiable desire for more and more stuff. The message is clear: you need to buy this to be happy, to fit in, to be successful. And before you know it, people are caught up in a cycle of buying things they don't really need, often going into debt just to keep up with these manufactured expectations.

Now, the work aspect of it can be equally troubling. Some companies demand long hours and intense workloads at the expense of personal time, family life and even mental health. It's as if they're sucking the soul out of their employees, expecting them to prioritize work above all else.

And then there are quick loans and credit cards, which can be a double-edged sword. On the one hand, they provide convenience but on the other, they can lead to financial entrapment. High-interest rates and hidden fees can easily spiral people into debt, making them feel like they're working just to pay off those debts, almost like a form of economic slavery.

Isn't it important to recognize these issues and advocate for a more balanced and ethical approach! Promoting mindful consumption, advocating for workers rights and encouraging financial literacy can help combat these exploitative practices and create a more equitable and compassionate society.

We have almost reached a place where there is no choice left, where there is no going back, the whole system is set up on top of that.

Your Journey

The road to wealth-building is not a sprint; it's a marathon. Each person's journey will be unique and it's essential to adapt your strategy to your specific circumstances and goals. Keep learning, stay disciplined and stay committed and over time you'll be well on your way to building your wealth. Let me break down some key ways to get started on your wealth-building adventure:

Creator Economy

The creator economy is booming, offering tremendous potential for individuals with passion and creativity. There will also come a time of saturation due to the low barrier of entry. From my personal experience speed and strategy matters most here. It's not a game of patience.

Building wealth in the creator economy – that's an exciting realm where anyone can leverage their skills, creativity and digital presence to make a living and in some cases make wealth. So, here's how you can make it happen:

First, discover your passion and expertise. Whether it's content creation, art, music, writing or any unique talent, pinpoint your niche and what sets you apart.

Your content is your currency. Deliver high-quality, engaging content consistently to attract and retain your audience. Content can be videos, articles, art, music or any form of digital creation.

Your personal brand is your identity in the creator economy. Craft a brand that reflects your personality and values. Consistency in branding is key to building trust and recognition. Identify your unique style within your creative field. This can set you apart from the competition and make your work more recognizable.

Interact with your followers. Respond to comments, host Q&A sessions and involve your audience in decisions. Building a loyal community can lead to ongoing support.

Explore multiple revenue streams. These might include ads, sponsorships, merchandise, affiliate marketing, subscriptions and direct donations from your fans.

Keep honing your skills and learning new ones. This ongoing self-improvement can help you stay at the top of your game.

By combining your talents with a solid business mindset, you can create wealth and make a living doing what you love. So, go out there and let your creativity shine!

If you're an artist, writer, designer, musician or any kind of creative, you can turn your passion into a source of wealth. It's not just about making money; it's about sharing your unique perspective and talents with the world. Establish an online presence through a website or social media. Share your work, engage with your audience and make it easy for people to find and contact you. Partner with brands or businesses that align with your creative style. Collaborations can lead to sponsored projects and increased exposure.

All the creative fields like art, music, acting, filmmaking, writing are moving into the creator economy. All in one.

Career

This is the easiest way to get started in your financial journey. Risk is low, reward may also be low here. But it can be a good way to learn industry skills and have financial stability or maybe a stepping stone to start a business and investments.

Start by investing in your education and skills. This might mean going to college, getting certifications or learning a trade. The more valuable your skills, the higher your earning potential. Have a holistic vision for your career.

Know where you want to go and what you want to achieve. Setting clear goals can help you stay motivated and focused. The job market is always evolving. Keep up with industry trends, new technologies and best practices to stay competitive and increase your earning potential.

By dedicating yourself to a specific field and continuously improving your skills, you can position yourself as a valuable specialist, attracting opportunities and financial success in your chosen domain.

Building wealth through specialization is a long-term commitment. It requires patience and persistence to become a recognized authority in your field. Specialists often command higher rates for their services. Don't undervalue your expertise; charge what your skills are worth. If you're in a service-oriented field, offer specialized services that cater to a niche market. Specialized services command higher rates.

In some specializations, creating and selling products can be lucrative. Develop unique products tailored to the needs of your specialized audience.

Consulting is a trillion dollar industry. Share your knowledge by offering consulting or coaching services. Many people are willing to pay for expert guidance in their specialized area of interest.

Building a strong professional network can open doors to new opportunities. Attend industry events, join professional organizations and connect with colleagues in your field.

Create a budget that allows you to save a portion of your income regularly. Make it a habit to pay yourself first by setting aside a percentage of your earnings for investments. Avoid lifestyle inflation when your income increases. Instead, save or invest the extra money, allowing your wealth to grow over time.

If you have a business idea or a side hustle that could generate extra income, explore the possibility of entrepreneurship. Starting a part-time business can supplement your career earnings. Over time, with the right strategies and a focus on growth, your career can become a significant source of wealth accumulation and financial security.

By design some people will make wealth through their career, most won't. It can also trap you forever as all your energy and time is spent dedicated only to serving the employer.

Investment

"Bulls make money, bears make money, pigs get slaughtered"

First they feed the pigs and their wealth flourishes during the bull markets. People indulge in lavish expenditures such as purchasing homes. Then the time comes to slaughter the pigs - bear markets, recessions and unemployment. During this time, they strip people of everything - their homes and vehicles, their happiness and aspirations.

That's why traditional wisdom matters. People will fool you by showing temporary proof of success. Most will fake it. Apply what passes the test of time.

Educate yourself about personal finance and investment. Understanding the fundamentals will help you make informed decisions and avoid costly mistakes. Investing in stocks, bonds and real estate can help your wealth grow over time. Compound interest is your best friend here! Stay informed. Research potential investments and consider taking courses or reading books about investing. Knowledge is a powerful tool. Some investments are riskier than others and you need to be comfortable with the level of risk in your portfolio. Generally, higher risk can mean higher potential returns but also greater potential losses.

Buy what's undervalued, Avoid what's overvalued. This is where the whole world can be a fool together, in masses.

Don't put all your eggs in one basket. Diversify your investments across different asset classes like stocks, bonds, real estate and even alternative investments like commodities or cryptocurrencies. Diversification helps spread risk.

Don't let market fluctuations rattle you. Volatility is part of the investment game. Stay focused on your long-term goals and avoid making impulsive decisions during market swings.

Investments are not for quick cash. Take a long-term view and be patient. Historically, the stock market, for instance, has shown solid long-term growth.

Be mindful of tax implications. Strategies like tax-loss harvesting and using tax-advantaged accounts can minimize your tax burden. You have to always do your research and any laziness will cost dearly.

Business

A lack of wealth keeps people working as employees. There are a million businesses you can start with money. A lot depends on wealth. A lot. World will fool you, they will tell you people don't start business because they can't take risks. But why can't they take risks? The number one reason people don't start business is nothing else but lack of money. Sure, great ideas and great minds can build great businesses but the reality is they work for others. People work jobs for money. They don't have enough to survive. Money matters. Many would-be entrepreneurs are held back by financial constraints. Starting a business often requires a significant initial investment and not everyone has access to that kind of capital. Economic instability or uncertainty can make people reluctant to start a business. A basic support system is important for entrepreneurs. Some people may not have the backing they need from family or friends to take the leap. You'll need startup capital. This might come from your savings, investments or even crowdfunding. Make sure you have enough financial resources to get your business off the ground.

Starting your own business can be a powerful wealth-building strategy. It's about supplying what the market demands. If there is no demand, there is no business. Understand your target market, competition and industry trends. It's a path you have to create. Use your compass of wisdom to adapt, evolve and move forward, there is no roadmap. Leverage of money, time and products is what builds wealth.

CHAPTER EIGHTEEN

NATIONS

A nation is a story of unity, diversity and shared purpose. It is a home for its people, a place where rights and responsibilities are honored and where the collective will of the citizens shapes its destiny.

It is a reflection of the human experience where differing voices and ideas may clash and where the pursuit of justice and progress is an ongoing journey. Like any living entity it has its moments of turmoil and transition.

It's people with their diverse backgrounds, traditions and beliefs are the heartbeats of this living entity. They are the authors of its ongoing narrative and the architects of its future.

What's makes nations great is the vibrant marketplaces where the commerce of ideas and goods unfolds, a necessity to the nation's vitality. The schools and universities where knowledge is cultivated, where the seeds of innovation are sown and the nation's intellectual legacy is nurtured.

Well, that's not always the case. A nation is built by its people and corruption is human nature. Nation is an organization for our survival and prosperity. Every organization is susceptible to corruption.

Game of Power

Remember you are not just a citizen, You can form a government.

We live in a world where governments, seduced by the intoxicating allure of dominion, use their authority to manipulate, surveil and exploit their own people. In this shadowed game of power, the rulers craft a narrative that justifies their actions, wrapping themselves in the guise of protectors and benefactors while covertly stifling dissent and amassing wealth at the expense of their citizens.

These governments, like puppet masters, pull the strings of their citizen's lives, dictating the paths they must tread, the thoughts they may harbor and the freedoms they can enjoy. They employ tools of control like censorship, propaganda and surveillance to keep their citizens in check.

As these authorities consolidate their power, they amass wealth and resources that should rightfully benefit the populace. Corruption thrives like a cancer, undermining the very foundations of justice and fairness. While the elites luxuriate in their opulence, the citizens suffer, struggling to make ends meet, their dreams and aspirations suffocated by avaricious rule.

The exploiters manipulate the very systems designed to protect the people. Laws become weapons used to quell dissent and perpetuate the status quo, while the legal system is twisted to shield those in power from accountability. Those who dare to challenge the regime are silenced, exiled or worse vanishing into the abyss of the government's retribution.

While there are leaders and individuals who wield their power with integrity, striving to serve the common good and protect the rights and dignity of their citizens.

The challenge lies in maintaining a vigilant society that demands transparency, accountability and ethical leadership. In this way power can be a tool for progress, justice and the collective welfare of the people, rather than a force for control and exploitation.

It is the collective duty of society to shape the nation, to ensure that power is a force that empowers and uplifts, rather than one that stifles and exploits its very lifeblood - its very own citizens.

People are the seeds of transformation, their ideas and actions growing into movements that blossom into societal shifts. Through art, culture, technology and community engagement, they challenge stereotypes and forge paths of understanding, paving the way for unity, innovation and progress.

The power of a better future lies not solely in the hands of politicians or leaders but in the collective will of individuals who are determined to shape a world where equality, justice and sustainable practices thrive. They understand that societal evolution is a journey and they are committed to taking that journey, no matter how long or winding the path may be. That is the kind of person we need to be in the society.

In the end, it is the passion, resilience and unity of people that can mold society, markets and nations into the better future we envision.

Your Journey

It's often said that power corrupts but what if I told you that power, when wielded by good people, can be a force for tremendous positive change in building a great nation. A nation benefits when its leaders are ethical and dedicated to the common good. The legacy they leave can shape the nation for generations to come. It's not just about power; it's about the kind of people who hold it and their commitment to building a nation that truly stands as a symbol of hope, progress and justice. And you should reconsider having an influence in this space.

Politics

Politics isn't just about politicians and government; it's the very essence of how we as a society make decisions and allocate resources.

Every law, every policy, every budget allocation and every decision that impacts our daily lives is a product of politics. Whether it's healthcare, education, the economy or even our rights and freedoms, politics is the driving force behind it all.

Politics also shapes our nation by defining our relationships with other countries. Foreign policy decisions, treaties and trade agreements are all outcomes of political processes that affect our global standing and how we interact with the rest of the world.

Politics influences the distribution of resources and opportunities within our society. It can either promote equity and social justice or perpetuate inequality, depending on the policies and decisions made.

It determines the direction we take, the values we uphold and the kind of society we become. So, whether you're an active participant or a concerned observer, understanding how politics shapes our nation is important for your life and your future generations.

Politics is the most powerful of all that shapes the collective destiny of the nation. Now it's your decision how you perceive politics and how you go forward with this. It's easy to blame and play victim but it takes guts to be a politician. It takes a different mindset. It takes a different approach. It takes a different skill set than you were taught in schools.

Political System Failure

If you live in a country where the political system isn't strong, you may be in big trouble soon. The political system failure in Pakistan is having a great impact on its citizens. The consequences of this failure are far-reaching and affect people's lives in numerous ways.

One of the most glaring issues is the lack of political stability. Frequent changes in leadership, corruption and power struggles within the government have left citizens grappling with uncertainty. When the political system is unstable, it becomes challenging to make long-term plans or investments in the country's future. Another major concern is the economic impact. Poor governance and corruption hinder economic development. As a result there are high levels of unemployment, inflation and a general lack of economic opportunities for the average citizen. The economic struggles of individuals and families are exacerbated by the failures of the political system.

The failure to provide essential public services, like education and healthcare, takes a toll on the everyday lives of the people. Many citizens in Pakistan do not have access to quality education and healthcare services, leading to a perpetuation of poverty and inequality. The political system failure also impacts the overall sense of security. Security issues, both internal and external, have a direct impact on the lives of ordinary citizens. Ongoing conflicts and instability can make people feel vulnerable and anxious about their safety.

The consequences of political system failure in Pakistan are not abstract issues. They affect the livelihoods, well-being and future prospects of their citizens.

Banking

Central banks are responsible for controlling a nation's money supply. They can increase or decrease the amount of money in circulation, which directly influences interest rates and inflation. These two factors, interest rates and inflation, affect everything from the cost of borrowing money to the purchasing power of our currency.

When a central bank adjusts interest rates, it can stimulate or cool down economic activity. Lower rates make borrowing cheaper, encouraging spending and investment, which can drive economic growth. On the other hand, raising rates can curb inflation and excessive borrowing, promoting economic stability.

Inflation control is another critical role of central banks. Excessive inflation can erode the value of our money, making it less valuable and impacting our savings and purchasing power. Central banks work to maintain a balance, ensuring that prices remain relatively stable.

Central banks also serve as lenders of last resort. In times of financial crisis, they step in to provide liquidity to banks and institutions that are struggling. This stabilizes the financial system and prevents widespread panic and economic collapse.

Additionally, central banks often manage a nation's foreign exchange reserves, which can impact exchange rates and international trade. By buying or selling foreign currency, they can influence the relative value of their nation's currency, affecting trade balances and the competitiveness of their country's exports.

Furthermore, central banks play a critical role in regulating and supervising financial institutions, which helps maintain the integrity of the banking system and protect consumers' deposits.

So, in a nutshell, central banks shape a nation's economic landscape. Their policies can influence growth, interest rates, inflation and even the stability of the financial system.

Most people don't realize but decisions of central banks directly impact you. They have the power to print a paper and call it money.

Financial System Failure

This thing can turn your money into just a piece of paper again. It happened, it's happening and it will happen one hundred percent. Because the whole system is designed for that to happen. The complete failure of a country's financial system can be absolutely devastating and we've seen this happen in various parts of the world.

Take Venezuela, for instance. Hyperinflation and economic mismanagement led to the devaluation of the country's currency. Citizens there experienced skyrocketing prices for basic goods, making it incredibly difficult for them to afford food, medicine and even daily necessities. Savings evaporated and people's purchasing power dwindled to almost nothing.

Take Zimbabwe. They went through a period of hyperinflation as well, where prices doubled multiple times a day. People had to carry huge bags of cash just to buy simple items. The financial system's failure eroded their savings and disrupted their lives.

In Greece, during the European debt crisis, austerity measures and economic instability caused immense hardships for citizens. Pensions were cut, businesses closed and unemployment rates soared, leaving many struggling to make ends meet.

And let's not forget the global financial crisis of 2008, which affected people not just in one country but worldwide. People lost their homes, jobs and savings. The failure of financial institutions had a ripple effect, impacting the everyday lives of millions. It leads to loss of wealth, diminished living standards and even social and political unrest. This is the hidden enemy that can attack anywhere, anyone. Be prepared.

Military

Military isn't just about soldiers and weapons; it's a force that molds the very identity and security of a country.

First and foremost, the military provides national defense like a shield protecting us from external threats and ensuring our sovereignty. Whether it's safeguarding our borders or responding to international crises, the military stands ready to protect our way of life. But it goes beyond that. The military also shapes our national identity. It embodies the values, courage and sacrifice that define our nation.

Military plays a pivotal role in times of disaster and crisis. Whether it's natural disasters, pandemics or other emergencies, the military is often called upon to provide aid, relief and support to affected areas. They're like a beacon of hope in our darkest hours.

Our military can also influence foreign policy and diplomacy. Its strength can serve as a deterrent, preventing potential adversaries from threatening us. And when diplomacy fails, it can be a powerful tool in advancing our national interests.

Military also contributes to technological innovation and economic growth. Research and development in defense-related fields have led to countless inventions and advancements that benefit our society as a whole.

Remember we are still in the jungle. International rules are superficial. There are no rules. Strong nations destroy weak nations. That's the reality. No matter how much progress and advancement we make, without strong military and defense powers it can be destroyed within days.

Military System Failure

When the military fails, we are back in the jungle where the strong will swallow the weak. If your military isn't strong, prepare for the day.

You know, the situation in Afghanistan and how the military failed to combat the Taliban is a topic that's been on many people's minds. It's a complex and sensitive issue but it's important to discuss.

They were up against a determined and well-organized insurgent group in the form of the Taliban. Over the years, the Taliban had gained significant support and control in various regions of Afghanistan, which made it even more challenging for the military to combat them effectively. The Afghan military faced shortages of essential supplies and lacked air support and intelligence capabilities, which put them at a significant disadvantage.

The abrupt withdrawal of international forces in 2021 left the Afghan military in a vulnerable position. They lost critical support and expertise and this sudden change in the situation had a demoralizing effect. The failure to combat the Taliban has had dire consequences for the Afghan people. It resulted in a swift takeover by the Taliban affecting millions of lives.

Judiciary

The judiciary, my friend, is like the guardian of justice in our nation. It plays a profound role in shaping our country and let me tell you, it's a role that's absolutely powerful and vital.

It ensures that the laws created by the legislature are in line with our Constitution, which is the bedrock of our democracy. When laws are challenged, it's the judiciary that steps in to decide if they're constitutional or not.

When there's a dispute, whether it's about individual rights, property, contracts or even government actions, people turn to the courts for resolution. Judges are supposed to make decisions based on the law and the Constitution, not on popular opinion or political affiliation. Their decisions reverberate through generations, influencing our culture, politics and how we live our lives.

Let me be frank with you - corruption within the judiciary is a cancer that destroys a nation from the inside out. When judges and court officials are susceptible to bribes and kickbacks, the decisions they make are no longer based on the merits of the case but on personal gain. This results in innocent people being wrongly convicted, while the guilty go free, creating a breeding ground for lawlessness and social unrest.

Civil Services

Civil services are responsible for implementing government policies and programs. They are the doers, the ones who take the laws passed by our elected representatives and put them into action. Whether it's ensuring the smooth operation of public services, managing public finances or regulating industries, civil servants are the ones making it happen.

They also act as a bridge between the government and the people. When you need information, services or assistance from your government, it's often a civil servant who provides that help. They are the face of government in your community, working to ensure that you receive the services you deserve.

Civil services are instrumental in maintaining continuity and stability in government. While elected officials may come and go, civil servants provide the institutional memory and expertise needed to keep government functioning effectively. They ensure that the policies enacted by one administration are smoothly transitioned to the next.

Moreover, they contribute to the development of public policy by providing valuable expertise and insights to the decision-makers. They conduct research, gather information and analyze trends, helping shape policies that address the nation's most pressing issues.

Civil servants also play a crucial role in upholding the rule of law. They are responsible for enforcing regulations, ensuring that businesses and individuals comply with the law and maintaining order and security in our communities.

Civil services are the backbone of our government, providing essential services, expertise and continuity. They are the gears that keep the machinery of our nation running smoothly.

When corruption takes root within the civil services, it destroys the society. It's as if a shadow is cast over the very institutions meant to serve and protect us.

Corruption diverts resources meant for public welfare into the pockets of a few. It's like a leak in the pipeline, draining funds that should be used for essential services like education, healthcare and infrastructure. As a result, the quality of these services deteriorates and the people suffer.

Investors are reluctant to engage in a nation where corruption is rampant as they fear unfair competition and a lack of transparency. This hampers economic development and job creation ultimately affecting the prosperity of the nation.

It can fuel social unrest, protests and in extreme cases lead to political instability. When people lose faith in the institutions meant to protect their rights, it can have dire consequences for the fabric of society.

So, if you're a good person, don't shy away from seeking power, for your vision and integrity can be the catalyst for a great nation.

Call to Action - World

Power & Control

Accept the imperfect, cooperate and serve the society.

Seek wealth, influence and power to save yourself from follies, exploitations and control of the world.

Use power to shape societies, religions, markets and nations for a better future.

IV. God : Pray & Meditate

God is Eternal.

Lastly, the God section is like a gentle breeze of hope and belief. The universe stretches before us an unexplored canvas full of mysteries. Prayer and meditation are like a soulful playlist that helps you tune into the rhythm of the divine.

LIFE

Life is a gift, Experience it.

When kids get their hands on a ball, they just play with it, right? They don't stop to think about who made the ball or whose ball it is. They simply enjoy it.

Well, life is a lot like that. It's a gift and you should experience it to the fullest. It doesn't matter who gave you this life; just play, live and experience it. Never, ever give up on life in the name of spirituality. Trust me, that would be a massive mistake, one that's often irreversible.

You see, some folks chase after God as if they were kids chasing after their daddy. But remember, a kid's job isn't to worship their daddy; it's to experience life.

There's nothing more meaningful than the life you have, so cherish it. Life is a gift and it's meant to be experienced. Don't sacrifice it for the pursuit of spirituality. Instead, respect and embrace the gift of life.

You are a life, nothing else, everything else is made up. Live your life, savor every moment and truly experience it.

My Role Model of Life

I was truly fortunate to have a remarkable role model in my early years, someone who left an indelible mark on my life – My Grandma's Brother. He was a force of nature, a man brimming with vitality and zest for life.

In his youth, he toiled diligently and amassed a substantial fortune through hard work and dedication. Later on he used to go on extensive journeys, leaving a lasting impression on everyone he encountered. He naturally commanded respect and served as the quintessential role model for living a fulfilling life.

He would rise way before the sunrise at 4AM, every single day. Then he would take a cold shower. While taking a cold shower he would mostly be chanting a simple one-word mantra. Then he would proceed to the farm temple for meditation, which, back in those days, wasn't referred to as "meditation" but as "Dhyan" in Hindi, closest in meaning to "focus" in English. In my village, we don't have temples in our homes; we have temples in our farms. He would spend around 30 minutes there in Dhyan and silently chanting a mantra.

The fascinating thing about his practice was that he didn't rely on the intricate logic we always demand in modern times. He simply did it, without the need for complex explanations. And even in this age of abundant information and knowledge, many of us fail to follow through with such simple, time-tested practices. There's a profound wisdom in doing things that have stood the test of time.

Believe me when I say, I have never encountered another individual as vibrant and full of life as he was. Not to this day. His way of life will always be an inspiration for me that life's true richness is found not in the acquisition of knowledge alone but in the pursuit of enduring, meaningful actions.

Meditation

Meditation is not something you want to be expert at, You want it to be part of your life. It doesn't have to be some intricate, complex practice that you need to study for years. In fact, there's one fundamental thing that truly matters - consistency.

The truth is, we all engage in a simplified form of meditation every day. Think about it, when your mind is at peace, your body follows suit. It could be as simple as closing your eyes, shutting out the noise of the outside world and focusing on your breath. That's meditation, right there.

Just sit in stillness, let go of your thoughts and just be. It's the purest and most effective form of meditation.

The key here is not to get caught up in mastering elaborate techniques. The real key is making it a part of your daily routine.

So, picture this: you wake up, get yourself ready and kickstart your day with a 15 to 30-minute session of prayer and meditation. And remember, it's not about making a racket; prayers are meant to be a serene, personal connection.

Prayer

Prayer, my friend, comes in many forms but for now let's focus on one particular kind:

When you truly desire something in life, it's not enough to just pray for it; you've got to put in the work. It's a simple concept, really.

If you pray for wisdom, you should also be willing to work hard to gain that wisdom. If success is your goal, well, success doesn't just fall into your lap; you've got to roll up your sleeves and work for it. And if you pray for good health, don't forget that a good diet and regular exercise go hand in hand with your prayers.

You see, if you pray for something but don't actively pursue it, it might mean you didn't really want it in the first place. Your prayer becomes a mere utterance, a lie.

Some might ask, "Why pray when you can just work for it?" Well, here's the thing about prayers.

In this modern world, people are often too quick to dismiss things without proper consideration. They're so clever that if they don't have an immediate, well-packaged explanation, they reject it outright. They don't bother to do the research and truly understand what they're rejecting.

When you're faced with something you don't know much about, take a moment to educate yourself. Only then can you make an informed decision to either accept or reject it. Ignorance should never be the basis for your choices.

Now, picture a big goal you're determined to achieve. You think about it constantly; you want it more than anything.

Prayer is a sacred act. It's a pure expression of your deepest desires. When you wish for something with a heart full of sincerity, all your energies become aligned toward that goal. It's a powerful force, indeed.

So, hold onto your faith and keep working toward your dreams. Who knows what extraordinary things might happen along the way?

CHAPTER TWENTY

NATURE

"The universe stretches before us an unexplored canvas full of mysteries."

You might have heard the story of a farmer and his lazy sons.

Once there lived a farmer in a village. He was very hardworking. He had made a good fortune with great toil and sweat over years. He had three sons, all of them healthy but quite lazy. This worried the farmer.

As the farmer grew old and sick, his sons continued to spend their days sleeping, eating and playing. He became more and more anxious about their future. He wanted his sons to take care of his fields as he did. One day, he gathered his sons and shared a secret with them, saying, "Dear sons, there's a lot of gold hidden in one of my fields to ensure you'll never go hungry."

After a few days, the farmer died and the sons were very sad for some time. After that, the sons decided to search for the gold which their father had told them about. Armed with their father's spades and mattocks, they dug up every inch of their fields in their quest to find it but their efforts yielded nothing.

A friend of their father saw this and suggested them to sow some seeds as they have already tilled the soil. The sons took this advice and started planting. Fortunately, the season brought ample rainfall. Days passed. The fields rewarded their labor with abundant crops that season. The sons were delighted to see crops swinging with the wind in their fields. The sons realized what was the hidden gold and said to each other "This is the gold our father wanted us to find".

God is like that gold in the fields, you can't find it but you can realize it.

We think so highly of ourselves that we forget the vastness of nature and the universe. What makes us so special is that we must seek God and other creatures don't have to. Isn't nature and the universe big enough to explore and discover? Aren't our lives interesting enough to enjoy and live fully? What is it that we seek God at the expense of what we have? We have a long enough life compared to most creatures whose life is in days. Those creatures live and die. Yet we desperately need a God and still not live a life fully. I find the solution is to explore and observe what is. You are. Nature is. Creatures are. Jungles are. Mountains are. Deserts are. Oceans are. Universe is. Earth is not fully explored, the Universe is not definitely explored. Why do we seek easy answers?

Observe the fellow creatures, believe it or not they are. Creatures of all sizes and shapes share this world, from the majestic to the minuscule. Eagles soar their wings outstretched in perfect harmony with the wind while ants labor in intricate societies beneath our feet. Birds sing with voices as diverse as a choir and squirrels play hide-and-seek among the branches. Bees buzz with purpose, ants build intricate cities underground and fireflies create enchanting displays of light in the night. From the tiniest insects to the mammals, they each bring their unique contributions to the intricate web of existence.

Observe the natural seasons, how effortlessly it happens. Nature's seasons mark the passage of time. Spring brings blossoms and the return of migratory birds. Summer bathes the world in warmth with lazy days and vibrant green landscapes. Autumn paints the trees in fiery hues and winter blankets the earth in a glistening snow and quiet. All of this is happening in an automated process while you were sitting there thinking about god and your life.

Climb the majestic mountains. It will bring some sense of how small we are. Mountains have long been revered by cultures around the world. People have always thought mountains are special and holy. They are often regarded as sacred places, inhabited by gods and are the settings for ancient myths and legends. Many pilgrims and adventurers have sought the solitude and spiritual inspiration that mountains provide. Harsh weather, avalanches and challenging terrain make mountaineering an endeavor that tests human strength and resilience. The allure of mountains is timeless and their grandeur continues to appeal to explorers and seekers both literally and metaphorically. They inspire people to reach new heights. Why not test yourself!

Spend time on the beaches and in the sea. Oceans cover more than 70% of Earth's surface and are the lifeblood of our planet. Stretching as far as the eye can see, the oceans are a study in contrasts. From the tranquil surface where the sun's golden rays create a shimmering expanse of blue, to the dark abyssal depths where pressure is crushing and light is scarce; oceans hold secrets and mysteries that challenge our understanding of the natural world. The oceans with their vast expanse and hidden depths are places of exploration and discovery, both for science and the human soul.

Face the Jungle. Our ancestors survived that. The jungle is a place of intense competition and collaboration. Face the terror of real jungle cats, tigers, jaguars and leopards. Countless species from the smallest insects to the largest mammals share these dense ecosystems. Insects scuttle beneath the fallen leaves while dart frogs display their vibrant colors as a warning to potential predators. Jungles are places of exploration and discovery where the frontiers of knowledge continue to expand.

Bear the Harsh weather of the desert. In the day, deserts are scorching crucibles where the sun's relentless rays turn the landscape into an oven of shimmering heat. Yet as the sun descends the desert transforms into a realm of enchanting coolness and breathtaking starry skies. Deserts are geologic masterpieces, shaped over millennia by wind, water and time. Canyons, carved by ancient rivers, cut deep into the earth. And salt flats stretch to the horizon. Plateaus rise with majestic solitude. Explore the universe. Build a rocket ship and launch yourself in space. Observable universe is so large, around 93 billion light-years, that if you travel at the speed of light, it will take you 93 billion years and maybe if you can survive that long, you will increase the observable limit. The universe is a vast and wondrous expanse that encompasses all of space, time, matter and energy. It is the ultimate playground of existence, containing everything we know and everything we have yet to discover.

Explore the self, we are, we exist and we don't know much about ourselves. Maybe the entire universe is within us. Remember if you have the seed, you can grow the entire forest. Truth is like the Seed.

CHAPTER TWENTY-ONE

GOD

Pray to talk, Meditate to listen.

Throughout history humanity has sought the origin of the universe. In this vast cosmic expanse, nobody possesses the definitive key to unlock the secrets of its genesis. The truth is we remain in the dark. The truth is nobody knows the source.

The universe with its boundless mysteries continues to elude our grasp. The universe is unexplored, Consciousness is unsolved, Source is unknown and Source of the source is unconceivable. We haven't done all the necessary work to find the source.

We don't have the patience of thousands of years. We don't think beyond our-self and our lifetime. We don't even have the patience to explore the self. We are confined to the narrow confines of our own self-interest and our brief lifetimes.

When we don't know the truth, we remain in the darkness. In the face of this profound ignorance, we dwell in the obscurity of the unknown. It's the hope and belief that can get us going in spite of darkness. It is our unfaltering hope and unwavering belief that propel us forward, guiding us through the shadows, inspiring us to continue our relentless pursuit for truth.

The concept of godly beings with human-like qualities offers a profound solace to the human spirit, even when we lack full knowledge of the ultimate source of all existence.

What if God is not some distant entity but rather the very essence woven into the fabric of the universe? What if God is synonymous with consciousness? What if God is inextricably linked with consciousness, interwoven with our very thoughts and awareness?

When you think about the vastness of the universe and the beauty of the nature, the mightiest emperors and the wealthiest billionaires seem to diminish into insignificance. There are far greater, mysterious, unknown and uncharted forces at work in the universe. There are definitely bigger forces at play.

In response to this awe-inspiring observation, we find ourselves presented with two compelling choices and the beauty lies in embracing both. We can choose to pray, to engage in dialogue with this divine presence and to meditate, to listen to the subtle whispers of the cosmos. Simultaneously we can embark on an incredible journey of discovery of self, consciousness, universe and the origin.

The path to understanding the unknown, the unexplored and the mysterious awaits those with the curiosity and courage to seek it.

Wheel of Time

दुःख में सुमिरन सब करे सुख में करे न कोय।
जो सुख में सुमिरन करे दुःख काहे को होय ॥
- कबीर दास जी

It's a verse (Doha) by Kabir Das Ji which can be translated as below but has deeper meaning than literal meaning, when you look at it in different aspects of your life, not just spiritual.

*In anguish everyone prays to Him, In joy does none
To One who prays in happiness, how can sorrow
come.*

In the good times, it's easy to question or even dismiss the idea of a higher power. But when life gets tough, when you're facing those storms that make you feel like a tiny speck in the vast cosmos, that's when many of us start searching for something to hold onto. It's those moments when you realize there are things out there, things beyond our control and we're left pondering the mysteries of life and death.

The truth is, none of us really have all the answers when it comes to the source, the God. That's where belief and hope comes into play. In those difficult times, when people are faced with bigger troubles, that's when most people turn to their faith and hope. In the end we all need something to lean on when the going gets tough.

In the darkest of moments, hope is the glimmer of light that breaks through the clouds, reminding us that even in the depths of despair, there is a chance for a brighter tomorrow. Hope is more than just wishful thinking. It's the unwavering belief that better days are ahead, even when the road seems rough and the odds are stacked against us. It's the driving force that inspires us to keep moving forward, to strive for our dreams and aspirations and to never give up, no matter how tough things may get. It's the fuel that propels us to overcome adversity, to conquer our fears and to face life's big challenges head-on.

Never underestimate the strength of hope, for it has the ability to move mountains, to mend broken hearts and to light up the world with its radiant glow. Hope is a beacon of possibility, a source of inspiration and a reminder that no matter how dark the night may seem, the dawn will always break and a new day will begin.

Whether you are a devoted follower or a seeker of truth, you should not forget to experience the life gifted to you. You will meet many spiritual people who have given up on the gift of life, beware of them, as they have forgotten themselves in the search of truth or devotion to god.

They don't value the very reason they came into existence. If everyone follows their path humanity will cease to exist after a generation. Many young people fall into the trap. Be spiritual but don't be blind. What's the hurry, it's a lifetime of journey.

Think holistically. Take a big-picture view. Life has its highs and lows. There are things you can control and there are things only God can control. Pray, Meditate & Experience Life.

Call to Action - God

Pray & Meditate

Pray & Meditate, Daily.

Life is a gift, Experience it.

Explore The Unexplored & Mysterious.

Conclusion

Life when lived holistically and honorably, becomes an extraordinary journey. It opens the door to authentic joy and purpose.

Life gains its richness in the bonds we forge with our loved ones. To provide and protect isn't merely a duty; it's our sacred commitment to the family.

While navigating the societal dynamics, Be an architect of positive change. Our actions shape the collective consciousness and destiny of the entire humanity.

Let this book be a catalyst for intentional living, a call to think deeply, love wholeheartedly, navigate wisely and find serenity in the prayers and meditation.

Acknowledgement

Think Life has been a very special project to document my wisdom on living a holistic and honorable life.

I would like to express my heartfelt gratitude to the following individuals for their unwavering support and patience during the writing of this book:

First and foremost, I extend my deepest appreciation to my beloved wife, Savitri, whose constant encouragement and understanding made it possible for me to immerse myself in the writing process.

I extend my sincere thanks to my son, Shiva and my nephew, Kamal, for their patience and the many moments they selflessly allowed me to dedicate to this project and I am proud of you.

I am thankful to my family, friends and readers. This book is as much yours as it is mine. Let's celebrate the joy of creation together.

Appreciation

Dear Remarkable Reader,

As you turn the final pages of the book, I extend my heartfelt gratitude for joining me on this intellectual voyage.

May you carry its lessons, inspirations and musings into your daily life. Your role in this intellectual adventure is to bring the masterpiece to life, turn the knowledge into wisdom and for that I am profoundly grateful.

With sincere appreciation,
Mukesh Daily
Author, "Think Life"

Recommendations

Grab these books and let your reading adventure begin! May your exploration be as enlightening as the revelations within these pages! Each book is a key to a different door. Open it and who knows what wonders you'll find?

1. The Room Where It Happened by John Bolton
2. Sapiens
3. Homo Deus
4. The Hero With A Thousand Faces by Joseph Campbell
5. Riders of the Purple Sage by Zane Grey
6. The Pilgrim's Progress by John Bunyan
7. The Brothers Karamazov by Fyodor Dostoevsky
8. The Idiot by Fyodor Dostoevsky
9. Crime And Punishment by Fyodor Dostoevsky
10. 1984 by George Orwell

Happy Reading!

About The Author

Hey there, It's Mukesh Daily! I'm all about that holistic vibe, embracing life without sticking to any labels. My journey involves capturing the beauty of my world through filmmaking, photography and storytelling, it's my way of painting life's moments.

I penned down this book to share some timeless wisdom from generations on living a holistic and honorable life. Dive into it, soak up the goodness and let it light up your path. Go on, live your best, fabulous life!

For more information, visit mukeshdaily.com

Your Notes

www.ingramcontent.com/pod-product-compliance
Lightning Source LLC
Chambersburg PA
CBHW021529150726
47990CB00006B/2163